A Practical Guide to

Child Nutrition

3rd Edition

Angela Dare
Margaret O'Donovan

Series Editor: Miranda Walker

 Nelson Thornes

First published in 1996 by:
Stanley Thornes (Publishers) Ltd

Second edition published in 2002 by:
Nelson Thornes Ltd

Third edition published in 2009 by:
Nelson Thornes Ltd
Delta Place
27 Bath Road
CHELTENHAM
GL53 7TH
United Kingdom

A catalogue record for this book is available from the British Library.

ISBN 978 1 4085 0484 0

Illustrations by Angela Lumley and Jane Bottomley
Page make-up by Northern Phototypesetting Co. Ltd, Bolton
Printed and bound in Spain by GraphyCems
Transferred to digital printing 2007
Front cover photograph © Soupstock/Fotolia

CONTENTS

INTRODUCTION

This is a fully revised and updated text, written primarily for students studying for all the CACHE, BTEC and NVQ courses. We feel it would be valuable in all Early Years settings and that it would serve as an *aide-mémoire* for both new and experienced staff.

The book is designed as an accessible resource to enable childcare workers to plan and provide healthy nutrition for infants and young children. The first two chapters provide the essential knowledge needed to understand nutrients and their specific functions, as well as the foods that form the basis of a well-balanced diet. You may find it useful to read these two chapters first. Further chapters cover nutrition for the developing child and special dietary needs and practices. Chapter 11 links food and nutrition to the Early Years Foundation Stage and Key Stages 1 and 2 of the National Curriculum. There is a glossary at the end of the book and all words included in this are emboldened in the text. There is also a list of useful contact addresses and websites.

We hope you will find this third edition of the book helpful.

Angela Dare
Margaret O'Donovan
Miranda Walker

ABOUT THE AUTHORS

Angela Dare and Margaret O'Donovan come from backgrounds of health visiting, midwifery and teaching. They worked together for many years at City and Islington College, London, on nursery nursing and other child-care courses. Margaret O'Donovan also taught for a number of years at The Chiltern College, Caversham. Angela Dare was for several years an External Moderator for CACHE courses.

Miranda Walker has worked with children from birth to 16 years in a range of settings, including her own nursery and out-of-schools clubs. She has inspected nursery provision for Ofsted, and has worked at East Devon College as an Early Years and Playworker lecturer and NVQ assessor and internal verifier. She is a regular contributor to industry magazines and an established author.

ACKNOWLEDGEMENTS

The authors and publishers are grateful for permission to reproduce the following material:

The Child Growth Foundation for the percentile charts on page 132 (the full range of nine percentile charts produced for the UK are obtainable from Harlow Printing, Maxwell Street, South Shields, Tyne and Wear NE33 4PU); © Crown, by permission of the Controller of Her Majesty's Stationary Office for Tables 1.2 and 1.3 from *The Manual of Nutrition* (tenth edition) on pages 5 and 6, and for Key Stage 1 and 2 information on pages 169–78 taken fom the website www.wiredforhealth; and the Qualification and Curriculum Authority and the Department for Children, Schools and Families for text from *Curriculum Guidance for the Foundation Stage* on pages 169–78.

The authors would also like to give special thanks to Aaquib, Camilla, Laura, Jordan and Sanna for allowing their photographs to be reproduced or used as references for the artists, and to Anna O'Brien for her advice and valuable recommendations.

1 *NUTRITION*

This chapter covers:
- **Definitions and terms**
- **The human alimentary and digestive system**
- **How food energy is produced in the body**

The majority of adults know what constitutes a healthy, balanced diet for them, but different dietary principles apply when providing food and drink for children. Childcare workers require a sound knowledge of nutrition and the importance of healthy food for children's health, growth and development. Balanced nutrition in childhood lays the foundations for future good health and sensible dietary choices.

Definitions and terms

To help your understanding of the terminology used in nutrition, in the first part of this chapter we explain common words and phrases, which you will hear your tutors use. Make sure you refer back to them as you progress through the other chapters of the book.

The tables on pages 5 and 6 will be useful when you prepare infant feeds and weaning foods, plan and prepare meals for children, and help them with shopping and cooking activities.

NUTRITION

Nutrition is the study of food and how it is used in the body.

FOOD

Food is any solid or liquid that nourishes the body by:
- providing warmth and **energy** to maintain body temperature, and keep all organs and muscles working properly
- providing new material for growth, including tissue for the brain and nervous system; organs such as the heart, liver, lungs and kidneys; muscle and bone structures; and the lining of the gut, lungs and blood vessels

■ maintaining, healing and renewing body tissues
■ keeping all the body processes, including the prevention of infection, in good order.

Habits, cultural patterns and family attitudes to food affect the variety and types of food eaten by children.

NUTRIENTS

Nutrients are the 'building blocks' of food that carry out the functions listed above. There are seven essential nutrients: **proteins**, carbohydrates, fats, vitamins, minerals, fibre and water. They each have a particular part to play in the growth and health of the body, and are described in detail in Chapter 2, pages 11–30.

MACRONUTRIENTS

Proteins, fats and carbohydrates are known as **macronutrients**. They have many different functions but they all provide energy. They are needed in relatively *large* amounts by the body and are measured in grams.

MICRONUTRIENTS

Vitamins and minerals are known as **micronutrients**. They do not supply energy and are needed in relatively *small* amounts by the body. They are measured in milligrams or micrograms.

ENERGY

Energy is the ability to do work. Just as a car needs petrol (energy) to make it go, so our bodies need food to produce the energy to keep us warm, active and healthy. Even during sleep, energy is needed to keep the heart pumping and all the other organs functioning normally. Importantly, children also need energy for *growth*. Most foods provide some energy, but the main suppliers are the macronutrients. The energy produced by food is released slowly into the body and is controlled by substances called **enzymes**.

MEASUREMENT OF ENERGY

The international measurement unit of energy (including food energy) is the **joule**. However, the older term **calorie** is more commonly recognised and used in the UK, and is the one used throughout this book.

The joule and the calorie are small units, so the terms kilojoule (1000 joules) and kilocalorie (1000 calories) are used by the Department of

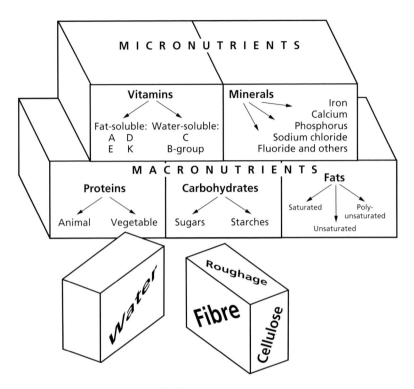

The essential nutritional building blocks

Health in the table of Estimated Average Requirements for energy (see page 6) and on the nutritional labels of packaged foods.

4.2 kilojoules (kJ) =   1 kilocalorie (kcal)
          1 g protein   provides   17 kJ/4 kcal
          1 g fat   provides   37 kJ/9 kcal
          1 g carbohydrate   provides   16 kJ/4 kcal

See Table 1.1 overleaf.

ENERGY REQUIREMENTS

Energy requirements vary according to age, gender and the amount of physical activity a person undertakes. People engaged in heavy physical work need more energy than office workers. Women tend to need less energy than men, although during pregnancy and lactation (breast-feeding), their energy requirements increase. Children and adolescents need a lot of energy because they are growing and active.

Table 1.1 Measurements used for food and nutrition

Energy

joule = J	1000 J = 1 kJ
kilojoule = kJ	4.2 kJ = 1 kcal
megajoule = MJ	1000 kJ = 1 MJ
kilocalorie = kcal	

Weight

microgram = μg	1,000,000 μg = 1 g
milligram = mg	1000 μg = 1 mg
gram = g	1000 mg = 1 g
kilogram = kg	1000 g = 1 kg
ounce = oz	16 oz = 1 lb
pound = lb	28 g = 1 oz
	100 g = 3.5 oz
	454 g = 1 lb
	1 kg = 2.2 lb

Liquid measure

fluid ounce = fl. oz	1000 ml = 1 l
pint = pt	20 fl oz = 1 pt
millilitre = ml	
litre = l	28 ml = 1 fl. oz
	568 ml = 1 pt
	1 l = 1.75 pt

DIETARY REFERENCE VALUES (DRVs)

These were published in 1991 by the Department of Health. They replace the former Recommended Daily Amounts (RDAs). DRVs refer to a range of daily nutrient requirements for different groups of individuals. They provide a guide when planning diets. There are three levels of intake:

■ **Estimated Average Requirement** (EAR) – this gives the *average* requirement for food energy or nutrient intake. Some people will need more and some less than this recommendation.

■ **Reference Nutrient Intake** (RNI) – this refers to the level of nutrient intake sufficient for almost every individual, even those with high nutritional requirements. These intakes will prevent nutritional disorders and, in children, promote normal growth.

■ **Lower Reference Nutrient Intake** (LRNI) – this is the amount set for the few individuals who have the lowest nutritional needs. Anyone constantly eating less than the LRNI will almost certainly become deficient in that nutrient.

It is important that energy intake (number of calories) is neither excessive nor inadequate for individual needs, so the recommendation for the different groups is set at the EAR.

See Table 1.2 below and 1.3 on page 6. These tables will be useful as a guide when you are planning children's meals.

ENZYMES

Enzymes are special proteins needed for all the chemical reactions that take place in the body. Digestive enzymes (juices) are made by the body in the salivary glands (in the mouth), and in the stomach, liver, pancreas and intestinal glands.

Table 1.2   Estimated Average Requirements for energy in the UK (per day)

Age range	Males		Females	
	MJ	kcal	MJ	kcal
0–3 months (formula fed)	2.28	545	2.16	515
4–6 months	2.89	690	2.69	645
7–9 months	3.44	825	3.20	765
10–12 months	3.85	920	3.61	865
1–3 years	5.15	1230	4.86	1165
4–6 years	7.16	1715	6.46	1545
7–10 years	8.24	1970	7.28	1740
11–14 years	9.27	2220	7.92	1845
15–18 years	11.51	2755	8.83	2110
19–50 years	10.60	2550	8.10	1940
51–59 years	10.60	2550	8.00	1900
60–64 years	9.93	2380	7.99	1900
65–74 years	9.71	2330	7.96	1900
75+ years	8.77	2100	7.61	1810
Pregnant*			+0.80	+200
Lactating				
1 month			+1.90	+450
2 months			+2.20	+530
3 months			+2.40	+570
4–6 months			+2.00	+480
>6 months			+1.00	+240

* Last trimester only.

Table 1.3 Reference Nutrient Intakes for selected nutrients for the UK (per day)

Age range	Protein (g)	Calcium (mg)	Iron (mg)	Zinc (mg)	Vitamin A (µg)	Thiamin (mg)	Vitamin B6 (mg[a])	Folic acid (µg)	Vitamin C (mg)
0–3 months (formula fed)	12.5	525	1.7	4.0	350	0.2	0.2	50	25
4–6 months	12.7	525	4.3	4.0	350	0.2	0.2	50	25
7–9 months	13.7	525	7.8	5.0	350	0.2	0.3	50	25
10–12 months	14.9	525	7.8	5.0	350	0.3	0.4	50	25
1–3 years	14.5	350	6.9	5.0	400	0.5	0.7	70	30
4–6 years	19.7	450	6.1	6.5	500	0.7	0.9	100	30
7–10 years	28.3	550	8.7	7.0	500	0.7	1.0	150	30
Males									
11–14 years	42.1	1000	11.3	9.0	600	0.9	1.2	200	35
15–18 years	55.2	1000	11.3	9.5	700	1.1	1.5	200	40
19–50 years	55.5	700	8.7	9.5	700	1.0	1.4	200	40
50+ years	53.3	700	8.7	0.5	700	0.9	1.4	200	40
Females									
11–14 years	41.2	800	14.8[b]	9.0	600	0.7	1.0	200	35
15–18 years	45.0	800	14.8[b]	7.0	600	0.8	1.2	200	40
19–50 years	45.0	700	14.8[b]	7.0	600	0.8	1.2	200	40
50+ years	46.5	700	8.7	7.0	600	0.8	1.2	200	40
Pregnant	+6.0	c	c	c	+100	+0.1[d]	c	+100	+10
Lactating:									
0–4 months	+11.0	+550	c	+6.0	+350	+0.2	c	+60	+30
over 4 months	+8.0	+550	c	+2.5	+350	+0.2	c	+60	+30

a Based on protein providing 14.7% of the EAR for energy.
b These RNIs will not meet the needs of approximately 10% of women with the highest menstrual losses, who may need iron supplements.
c No increment.
d Last trimester only.

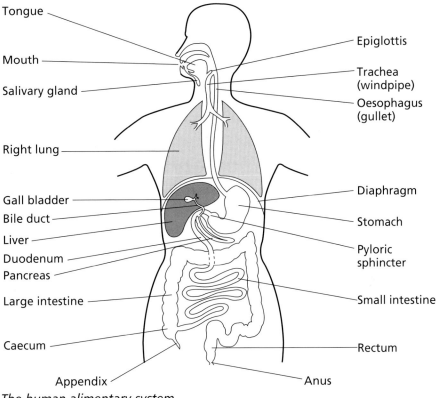

Tongue

Mouth

Salivary gland

Right lung

Gall bladder

Bile duct

Liver

Duodenum

Pancreas

Large intestine

Caecum

Appendix

Epiglottis

Trachea
(windpipe)

Oesophagus
(gullet)

Diaphragm

Stomach

Pyloric
sphincter

Small intestine

Rectum

Anus

The human alimentary system

METABOLISM

Metabolism describes all the changes that take place in the body to do with food and the use of energy.

FOOD STANDARDS AGENCY (FSA)

The Food Standards Agency came into effect in April 2000 under the Food Standards Act of November 1999. It is the responsibility of the **FSA** to protect consumers' rights and interests in relation to food quality and safety. The Agency acts independently and makes public any advice it gives to the government.

SCIENTIFIC ADVISORY COMMITTEE ON NUTRITION (SACN)

The Scientific Advisory Committee on Nutrition supports the Food Standards Agency. It offers good quality, independent advice to the

Department of Health and the Food Standards Agency on healthy eating and balanced diets; conditions in which nutritional status is a risk factor, for example, heart disease, some cancers, obesity and osteoporosis; and the effects of poverty and poor nutritional intake on the health, growth and development of children. One significant research conclusion is the importance of fortifying flour with folic acid to prevent neural tube defects in the developing baby during pregnancy.

The human alimentary and digestive system

The alimentary canal is a long muscular tube through which food passes. It is made up of the mouth, the oesophagus (gullet), the stomach, the small and large intestines, the rectum and the anus. Digestive juices are secreted into the alimentary canal to break up and digest food ready for absorption into the bloodstream.

WHAT HAPPENS TO FOOD WHEN WE EAT IT?

In the mouth
Chewing breaks the food into small pieces. At the same time, it is mixed with saliva from the salivary glands to form a bolus (soft mass of chewed food), which is then swallowed. Swallowing pushes the food down the oesophagus into the stomach.

In the stomach
Food is changed and partly digested by the action of gastric juices. It then leaves the stomach through the pyloric sphincter (a ring of muscle), which is normally closed but opens at intervals to let the food through, a little at a time, into the small intestine.

In the small intestine
Further digestion takes place here as digestive juices from the pancreas, gall bladder and intestine are mixed with the food. The food is then absorbed into the body through the walls of the small intestine. Materials remaining after absorption pass into the large intestine.

In the large intestine
The material here is mainly water, fibre and bacteria. Water and any useful substances remaining from food residue are absorbed. The remainder

(fibre, dead cells and bacteria) form the faeces. Peristaltic action moves the faeces into the rectum and out of the body via the anus.

(Peristalsis describes the wave-like contraction and relaxation movements of the small and large intestines, which help the digestion and absorption of food and the expulsion of faeces from the body.)

How food energy is produced in the body

CARBOHYDRATES

Carbohydrates (sugars and starches) are absorbed into the body as glucose. Glucose provides the body with energy. Some glucose circulates in the bloodstream to provide instant energy. Most is stored in the liver and muscles as **glycogen**, which can be broken down as necessary and converted back into glucose for use by the body as energy. Excess glucose is stored as fat in the fatty tissue of the body.

FATS

Fats are absorbed into the body as fatty acids and glycerol. These are used by the body to provide, among other things, energy for warmth, growth and work. Those not required for immediate 'fuel' are stored as fatty tissue that can be converted into energy as necessary.

PROTEIN

Excess protein *cannot* be stored as such in the body so, once its main functions have been carried out, any that is left over is converted into:
- energy for immediate use or stored energy in the form of glycogen or fat
- urea, a waste product excreted by the kidneys.

QUICK CHECK

1 What are:
   (a) nutrients?
   (b) macronutrients?
   (c) micronutrients?
2 Name the seven essential nutrients.
3 (a) What is energy?
   (b) How is it measured?
4 How is energy used in the body?

5 Why do children need a lot of energy?
6 How many grams are there in:
   (a) 1 oz?
   (b) 1 lb?
7 How many millilitres are there in:
   (a) 1 fl. oz?
   (b) 1 pt?
8 What do you understand by the following terms:
   (a) Dietary Reference Values?
   (b) Reference Nutrient Intake?
9 (a) What are enzymes?
   (b) Where in the body are digestive enzymes made?
10 In which part of the intestine does absorption of food take place?
11 What is peristalsis?
12 What is the end product of carbohydrate digestion?
13 (a) What is glycogen?
   (b) Where in the body is it stored?
14 How is excess glucose stored in the body?
15 What happens to excess protein in the body?

KEY WORDS AND TERMS

You need to know what these words and phrases mean. Go back through the chapter and find out.

calorie	joule
Dietary Reference Values	macronutrients
energy	metabolism
enzymes	micronutrients
food	nutrients
FSA	SACN
glycogen	

THE ESSENTIAL NUTRIENTS

> **This chapter covers:**
> ■ The role of the essential nutrients
> ■ The food groups
> ■ Dairy, staple and fortified foods

The role of the essential nutrients

Information about the seven essential nutrients is set out in the charts on pages 17–23, and in Tables 2.1 and 2.2 on pages 24–27. Try to look at these frequently, together with the text below – this will help you to gain a thorough understanding of nutrients.

PROTEIN

Protein is essential for building, repairing and maintaining body cells and tissues, and is particularly important for children's growth. No other nutrient can supply the necessary material for growth. Protein is also needed to make antibodies and enzymes.

Protein is composed of **amino acids**, some of which are made in the body. Others, known as essential amino acids, have to be taken in through food. Animal protein provides all the essential amino acids and is said to be of **high biological value** (HBV). Vegetable/plant protein, which contains only some of the essential amino acids, has a **low biological value** (LBV). LBV foods should be eaten in a variety of combinations and mixtures to ensure all the essential amino acids are obtained – this is known as **protein complementation** (see the chart on page 17 and the diagrams on pages 12, 13 and 16).

FATS

Fats are a concentrated form of energy. They also provide warmth and protect organs such as the heart and kidneys. Food is made more palatable by the addition of fat – think how much more tasty a slice of bread or toast is, if it is spread with butter or margarine, rather than eaten dry.

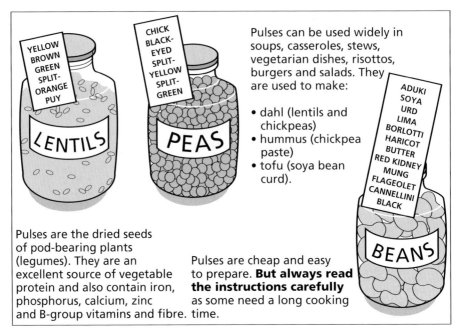

YELLOW
BROWN
GREEN
SPLIT-
ORANGE
PUY

CHICK
BLACK-
EYED
SPLIT-
YELLOW
SPLIT-
GREEN

Pulses can be used widely in soups, casseroles, stews, vegetarian dishes, risottos, burgers and salads. They are used to make:

ADUKI
SOYA
URD
LIMA
BORLOTTI
HARICOT
BUTTER
RED KIDNEY
MUNG
FLAGEOLET
CANNELLINI
BLACK

- dahl (lentils and chickpeas)
- hummus (chickpea paste)
- tofu (soya bean curd).

LENTILS

PEAS

BEANS

Pulses are the dried seeds of pod-bearing plants (legumes). They are an excellent source of vegetable protein and also contain iron, phosphorus, calcium, zinc and B-group vitamins and fibre.

Pulses are cheap and easy to prepare. **But always read the instructions carefully** as some need a long cooking time.

Pulses – vegetable/plant protein

Depending on their chemical composition, fats are either **saturated**, unsaturated or **polyunsaturated**. Many people eat too much saturated fat, which is high in cholesterol (see below) and carries the risk of health problems. Polyunsaturated fats are low in cholesterol and contain essential fatty acids (**EFAs**), which are very important for good health. EFAs cannot be made in the body so must be obtained through the diet. They are found in foods such as oily fish, soya products, nuts and seeds, polyunsaturated margarines and oils such as corn, sunflower and groundnut.

While adults may be advised to reduce their total fat intake, children need fat in their diet, both as a source of energy and for the fat-soluble vitamins A and D, which are found mainly in animal fats.

CHOLESTEROL

Cholesterol is an important fat-like substance made naturally in the body and also obtained from animal products, such as egg yolk, fatty meat and meat products, such as sausages, bacon, ham, liver sausage, black pudding, salami and polony, also butter, cream, dripping and lard, hard cheeses, shrimps and prawns. Cholesterol is used to make cell membranes and the covering of nerve fibres. It also helps digestion of fats and the production of male and female sex hormones.

Too much saturated fat in the diet raises the level of cholesterol in the body and increases the risk of coronary heart disease and obesity – common health problems in affluent societies where there is a high intake of animal fats. Polyunsaturated fats help to lower the cholesterol level in the body (see the chart on page 18).

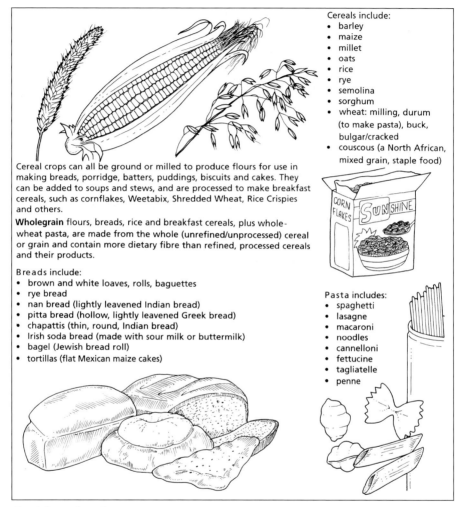

Cereals include:
- barley
- maize
- millet
- oats
- rice
- rye
- semolina
- sorghum
- wheat: milling, durum (to make pasta), buck, bulgar/cracked
- couscous (a North African, mixed grain, staple food)

Cereal crops can all be ground or milled to produce flours for use in making breads, porridge, batters, puddings, biscuits and cakes. They can be added to soups and stews, and are processed to make breakfast cereals, such as cornflakes, Weetabix, Shredded Wheat, Rice Crispies and others.

Wholegrain flours, breads, rice and breakfast cereals, plus whole-wheat pasta, are made from the whole (unrefined/unprocessed) cereal or grain and contain more dietary fibre than refined, processed cereals and their products.

Breads include:
- brown and white loaves, rolls, baguettes
- rye bread
- nan bread (lightly leavened Indian bread)
- pitta bread (hollow, lightly leavened Greek bread)
- chapattis (thin, round, Indian bread)
- Irish soda bread (made with sour milk or buttermilk)
- bagel (Jewish bread roll)
- tortillas (flat Mexican maize cakes)

Pasta includes:
- spaghetti
- lasagne
- macaroni
- noodles
- cannelloni
- fettucine
- tagliatelle
- penne

Cereals and grains

CARBOHYDRATES

Carbohydrates are divided into starches and sugars, and provide the body with energy and warmth. They are grouped, according to their chemical composition, into monosaccharides, disaccharides and polysaccharides.

Starchy carbohydrate foods, such as different breads, cereals, rice, pasta and starchy vegetables (see the diagrams above and on page 15), are not only high-calorie foods, but also contain other essential nutrients, including vitamins, minerals and fibre. They are relatively cheap and filling. Wholegrain breads, rice and pasta are higher in fibre than white equivalents. Starchy vegetables, such as cassava (manioc), sweet potatoes, yams and plantains (technically fruit but referred to as vegetable), are **staple foods** of West Indian, Asian and African diets, but are readily available in the UK and enjoyed by people of many cultures. Cassava, a root vegetable, is usually washed, dried, grated and used as a thickener in the same way as arrowroot. Plantains contain similar amounts of energy as potatoes and must be cooked well before eating.

Sugars are high in calories. Natural (intrinsic) sugar is found in milk, fruit and many vegetables, such as peas, carrots, parsnips, plantain, sweet potato, red peppers and red kidney beans. Processed, added (extrinsic) sugars are manufactured from sugar cane and sugar beet plants. They include white and brown table sugars, preserving and icing sugars, and those added to a wide range of foods and soft drinks. Extrinsic sugars are often referred to as single nutrient foods, providing '**empty calories**' – that means they provide only calories but little else of nutrient value. (Sugar and tooth decay is discussed in Chapter 8, pages 135–9.)

Dietary fibre, also known as '**unavailable carbohydrate**', is discussed on page 15. The chart on page 19 describes carbohydrates in detail.

VITAMINS

Vitamins are identified by letters, but some also have chemical names. Although they are only needed in small amounts by the body, vitamins are essential for health. Inadequate intake can lead to deficiency disorders, such as scurvy and rickets, and also to poor growth and health.

Some vitamins, for example vitamins C and D, have a specific role in helping the absorption of other essential nutrients. Some, namely vitamins A, D, E and K are fat-soluble, which means they *can* be stored in the body. Others, B-group and C vitamins, are water-soluble, which means they *cannot* be stored in the body and are easily destroyed by cooking – foods containing these vitamins need to be eaten daily.

Vitamins, with the exception of D and K, cannot be made in the body and must be taken in through food or vitamin supplements (see the chart on page 20 and Table 2.1 on pages 24–5).

MINERALS

Like vitamins, minerals are essential for health. They are provided by food or in the form of supplements. Minerals are classed as major minerals or

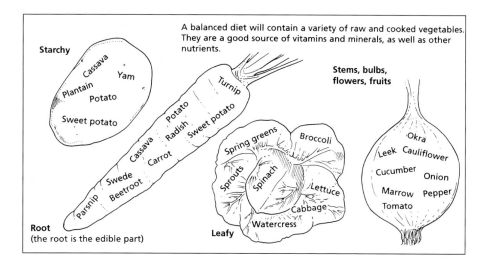

Vegetables grouped according to structure

trace elements according to amount needed by the body. Important major minerals are iron, sodium (usually called salt), potassium, calcium and phosphorus. Iron is important for the formation of **haemoglobin** in the red blood cells and transporting oxygen round the body. Lack of iron leads to iron-deficiency anaemia. Sodium and potassium are essential for maintaining fluid balance in the body, while calcium and phosphorus are necessary for strong and healthy bones and teeth.

Trace elements are only needed in very small amounts. **Fluoride** is probably the best known of the trace elements for its role in helping to prevent tooth decay.

For mineral requirements, see the chart on page 21 and Table 2.2 (pages 26–7).

DIETARY FIBRE

Dietary fibre is a non-starch polysaccharide. It is not digested and absorbed by humans, has no nutrient or calorific value and is referred to as 'unavailable carbohydrate'. However, it is classed as a nutrient in this book and appears on the nutrient diagram on page 3 because of its overall importance in aiding digestion and absorption of food. It encourages chewing and healthy gums and jaws, as well as promoting bowel health and preventing constipation (see the chart on page 22).

WATER

We cannot live without water. While people can survive for many weeks fasting from solids but taking in fluids, death would occur within a matter of days if water was not available. The kidneys regulate the water balance in the body, and urine output is a good guide to fluid intake and kidney function. **Dehydration** occurs when there is insufficient water in the body. Some causes of dehydration are outlined in Chapter 3, page 40.

For more information about water, see the chart on page 23.

NUTS AND SEEDS

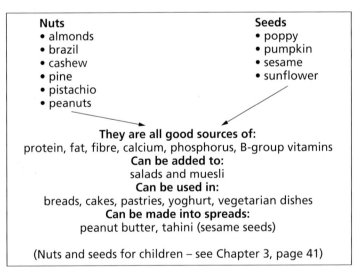

Nuts
- almonds
- brazil
- cashew
- pine
- pistachio
- peanuts

Seeds
- poppy
- pumpkin
- sesame
- sunflower

They are all good sources of:
protein, fat, fibre, calcium, phosphorus, B-group vitamins
Can be added to:
salads and muesli
Can be used in:
breads, cakes, pastries, yoghurt, vegetarian dishes
Can be made into spreads:
peanut butter, tahini (sesame seeds)

(Nuts and seeds for children – see Chapter 3, page 41)

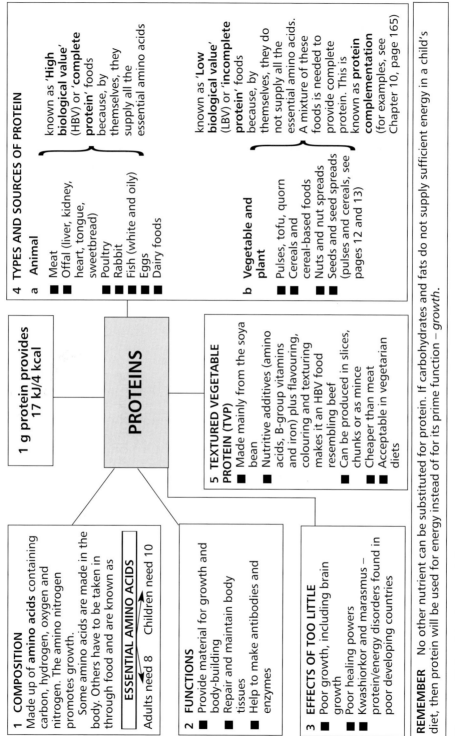

PROTEINS

1 g protein provides 17 kJ/4 kcal

4 TYPES AND SOURCES OF PROTEIN

a Animal
- Meat
- Offal (liver, kidney, heart, tongue, sweetbread)
- Poultry
- Rabbit
- Fish (white and oily)
- Eggs
- Dairy foods

known as 'High biological value' (HBV) or 'complete protein' foods because, by themselves, they supply all the essential amino acids

b Vegetable and plant
- Pulses, tofu, quorn
- Cereals and cereal-based foods
- Nuts and nut spreads
- Seeds and seed spreads (pulses and cereals, see pages 12 and 13)

known as 'Low biological value' (LBV) or 'incomplete protein' foods because, by themselves, they do not supply all the essential amino acids. A mixture of these foods is needed to provide complete protein. This is known as protein complementation (for examples, see Chapter 10, page 165)

5 TEXTURED VEGETABLE PROTEIN (TVP)
- Made mainly from the soya bean
- Nutritive additives (amino acids, B-group vitamins and iron) plus flavouring, colouring and texturing makes it an HBV food resembling beef
- Can be produced in slices, chunks or as mince
- Cheaper than meat
- Acceptable in vegetarian diets

1 COMPOSITION
Made up of **amino acids** containing carbon, hydrogen, oxygen and nitrogen. The amino nitrogen promotes growth.

Some amino acids are made in the body. Others have to be taken in through food and are known as

ESSENTIAL AMINO ACIDS

Adults need 8 → Children need 10

2 FUNCTIONS
- Provide material for growth and body-building
- Repair and maintain body tissues
- Help to make antibodies and enzymes

3 EFFECTS OF TOO LITTLE
- Poor growth, including brain growth
- Poor healing powers
- Kwashiorkor and marasmus – protein/energy disorders found in poor developing countries

REMEMBER No other nutrient can be substituted for protein. If carbohydrates and fats do not supply sufficient energy in a child's diet, then protein will be used for energy instead of for its prime function – *growth*.

The essential nutrients – proteins

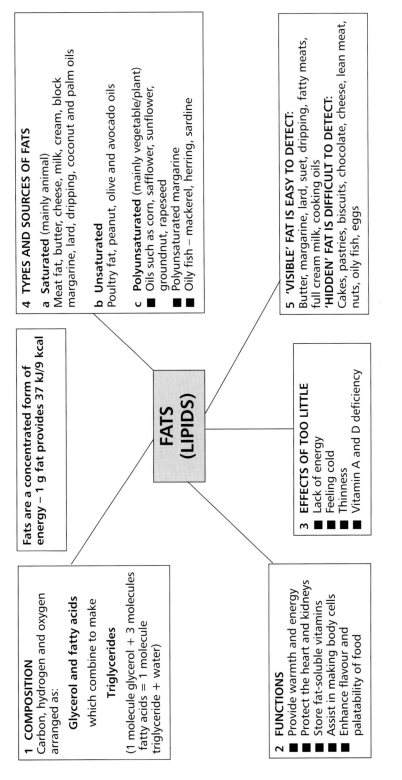

1 COMPOSITION
Carbon, hydrogen and oxygen arranged as:

Glycerol and fatty acids

which combine to make

Triglycerides

(1 molecule glycerol + 3 molecules fatty acids = 1 molecule triglyceride + water)

Fats are a concentrated form of energy – 1 g fat provides 37 kJ/9 kcal

4 TYPES AND SOURCES OF FATS

a Saturated (mainly animal)
Meat fat, butter, cheese, milk, cream, block margarine, lard, dripping, coconut and palm oils

b Unsaturated
Poultry fat, peanut, olive and avocado oils

c Polyunsaturated (mainly vegetable/plant)
■ Oils such as corn, safflower, sunflower, groundnut, rapeseed
■ Polyunsaturated margarine
■ Oily fish – mackerel, herring, sardine

FATS (LIPIDS)

5 'VISIBLE' FAT IS EASY TO DETECT:
Butter, margarine, lard, suet, dripping, fatty meats, full cream milk, cooking oils
'HIDDEN' FAT IS DIFFICULT TO DETECT:
Cakes, pastries, biscuits, chocolate, cheese, lean meat, nuts, oily fish, eggs

2 FUNCTIONS
■ Provide warmth and energy
■ Protect the heart and kidneys
■ Store fat-soluble vitamins
■ Assist in making body cells
■ Enhance flavour and palatability of food

3 EFFECTS OF TOO LITTLE
■ Lack of energy
■ Feeling cold
■ Thinness
■ Vitamin A and D deficiency

REMEMBER
Too much fat in the diet will lead to obesity and other health problems.

The essential nutrients – fats

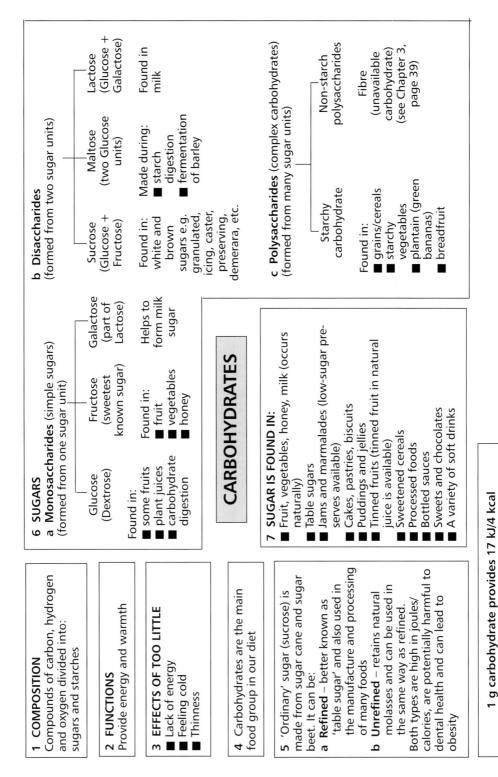

CARBOHYDRATES

1 COMPOSITION
Compounds of carbon, hydrogen and oxygen divided into: sugars and starches

2 FUNCTIONS
Provide energy and warmth

3 EFFECTS OF TOO LITTLE
- Lack of energy
- Feeling cold
- Thinness

4 Carbohydrates are the main food group in our diet

5 'Ordinary' sugar (sucrose) is made from sugar cane and sugar beet. It can be:
a Refined – better known as 'table sugar' and also used in the manufacture and processing of many foods
b Unrefined – retains natural molasses and can be used in the same way as refined.
Both types are high in joules/calories, are potentially harmful to dental health and can lead to obesity

6 SUGARS
a Monosaccharides (simple sugars) (formed from one sugar unit)

Glucose (Dextrose)	Fructose (sweetest known sugar)	Galactose (part of Lactose)
Found in: - some fruits - plant juices - carbohydrate digestion	Found in: - fruit - vegetables - honey	Helps to form milk sugar

b Disaccharides (formed from two sugar units)

Sucrose (Glucose + Fructose)	Maltose (two Glucose units)	Lactose (Glucose + Galactose)
Found in: white and brown sugars e.g. granulated, icing, caster, preserving, demerara, etc.	Made during: - starch digestion - fermentation of barley	Found in milk

c Polysaccharides (complex carbohydrates) (formed from many sugar units)

Starchy carbohydrate	Non-starch polysaccharides
Found in: - grains/cereals - starchy vegetables - plantain (green bananas) - breadfruit	Fibre (unavailable carbohydrate) (see Chapter 3, page 39)

7 SUGAR IS FOUND IN:
- Fruit, vegetables, honey, milk (occurs naturally)
- Table sugars
- Jams and marmalades (low-sugar pre-serves available)
- Cakes, pastries, biscuits
- Puddings and jellies
- Tinned fruits (tinned fruit in natural juice is available)
- Sweetened cereals
- Processed foods
- Bottled sauces
- Sweets and chocolates
- A variety of soft drinks

1 g carbohydrate provides 17 kJ/4 kcal

The essential nutrients – carbohydrates

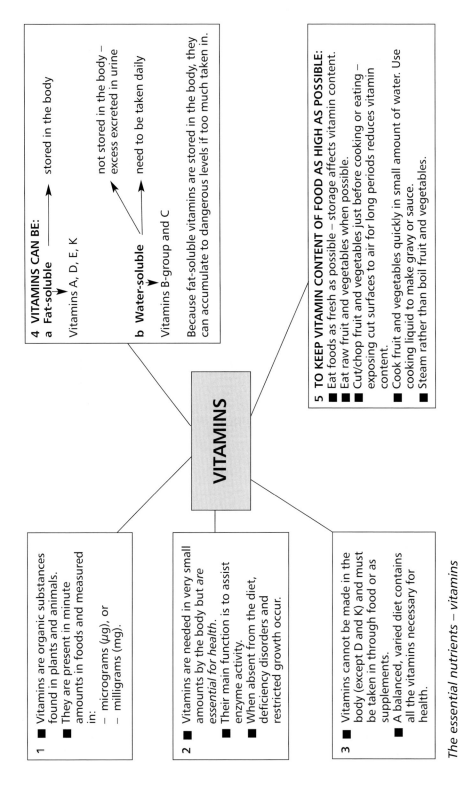

VITAMINS

1
- Vitamins are organic substances found in plants and animals.
- They are present in minute amounts in foods and measured in:
  - micrograms (μg), or
  - milligrams (mg).

2
- Vitamins are needed in very small amounts by the body but are *essential for health*.
- Their main function is to assist enzyme activity.
- When absent from the diet, deficiency disorders and restricted growth occur.

3
- Vitamins cannot be made in the body (except D and K) and must be taken in through food or as supplements.
- A balanced, varied diet contains all the vitamins necessary for health.

4 VITAMINS CAN BE:
a Fat-soluble → stored in the body

Vitamins A, D, E, K

b Water-soluble → not stored in the body – excess excreted in urine → need to be taken daily

Vitamins B-group and C

Because fat-soluble vitamins are stored in the body, they can accumulate to dangerous levels if too much taken in.

5 TO KEEP VITAMIN CONTENT OF FOOD AS HIGH AS POSSIBLE:
- Eat foods as fresh as possible – storage affects vitamin content.
- Eat raw fruit and vegetables when possible.
- Cut/chop fruit and vegetables just before cooking or eating – exposing cut surfaces to air for long periods reduces vitamin content.
- Cook fruit and vegetables quickly in small amount of water. Use cooking liquid to make gravy or sauce.
- Steam rather than boil fruit and vegetables.

The essential nutrients – vitamins

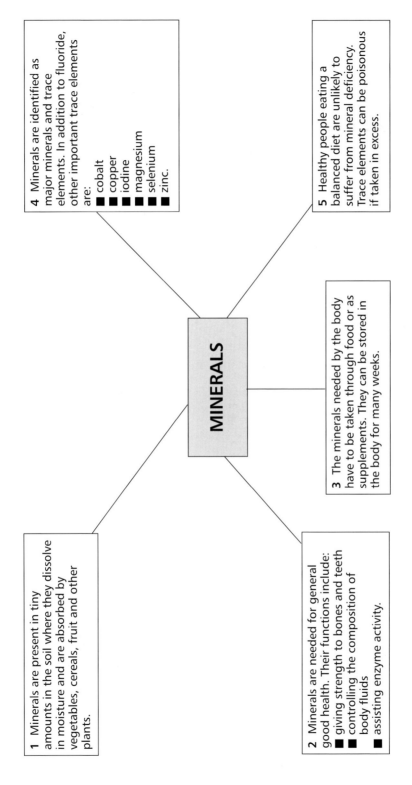

MINERALS

1 Minerals are present in tiny amounts in the soil where they dissolve in moisture and are absorbed by vegetables, cereals, fruit and other plants.

2 Minerals are needed for general good health. Their functions include:
- giving strength to bones and teeth
- controlling the composition of body fluids
- assisting enzyme activity.

3 The minerals needed by the body have to be taken through food or as supplements. They can be stored in the body for many weeks.

4 Minerals are identified as major minerals and trace elements. In addition to fluoride, other important trace elements are:
- cobalt
- copper
- iodine
- magnesium
- selenium
- zinc.

5 Healthy people eating a balanced diet are unlikely to suffer from mineral deficiency. Trace elements can be poisonous if taken in excess.

The essential nutrients – minerals

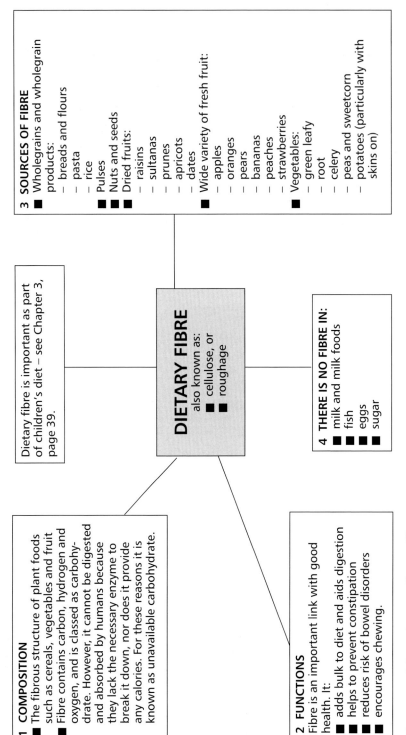

1 COMPOSITION
- The fibrous structure of plant foods such as cereals, vegetables and fruit
- Fibre contains carbon, hydrogen and oxygen, and is classed as carbohydrate. However, it cannot be digested and absorbed by humans because they lack the necessary enzyme to break it down, nor does it provide any calories. For these reasons it is known as unavailable carbohydrate.

Dietary fibre is important as part of children's diet – see Chapter 3, page 39.

DIETARY FIBRE
also known as:
- cellulose, or
- roughage

3 SOURCES OF FIBRE
- Wholegrains and wholegrain products:
  - breads and flours
  - pasta
  - rice
- Pulses
- Nuts and seeds
- Dried fruits:
  - raisins
  - sultanas
  - prunes
  - apricots
  - dates
- Wide variety of fresh fruit:
  - apples
  - oranges
  - pears
  - bananas
  - peaches
  - strawberries
- Vegetables:
  - green leafy
  - root
  - celery
  - peas and sweetcorn
  - potatoes (particularly with skins on)

4 THERE IS NO FIBRE IN:
- milk and milk foods
- fish
- eggs
- sugar

2 FUNCTIONS
Fibre is an important link with good health. It:
- adds bulk to diet and aids digestion
- helps to prevent constipation
- reduces risk of bowel disorders
- encourages chewing.

The essential nutrients – dietary fibre

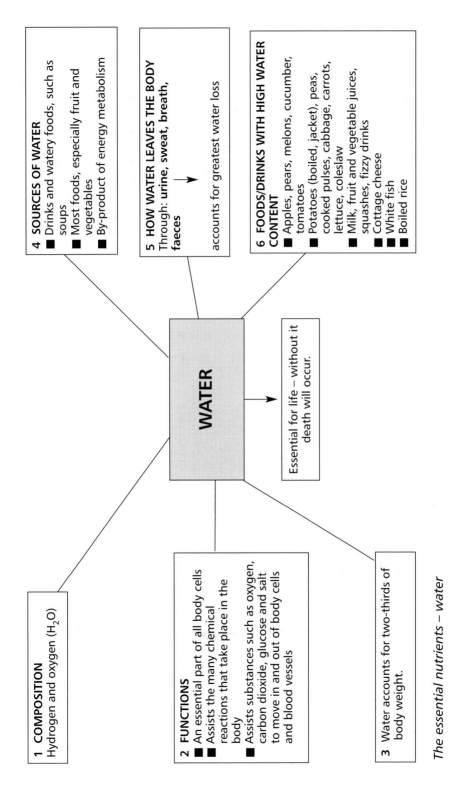

1 COMPOSITION
Hydrogen and oxygen (H_2O)

2 FUNCTIONS
- An essential part of all body cells
- Assists the many chemical reactions that take place in the body
- Assists substances such as oxygen, carbon dioxide, glucose and salt to move in and out of body cells and blood vessels

3 Water accounts for two-thirds of body weight.

WATER

Essential for life – without it death will occur.

4 SOURCES OF WATER
- Drinks and watery foods, such as soups
- Most foods, especially fruit and vegetables
- By-product of energy metabolism

5 HOW WATER LEAVES THE BODY
Through: **urine, sweat, breath, faeces**

accounts for greatest water loss

6 FOODS/DRINKS WITH HIGH WATER CONTENT
- Apples, pears, melons, cucumber, tomatoes
- Potatoes (boiled, jacket), peas, cooked pulses, cabbage, carrots, lettuce, coleslaw
- Milk, fruit and vegetable juices, squashes, fizzy drinks
- Cottage cheese
- White fish
- Boiled rice

The essential nutrients – water

Table 2.1 Vitamins

Name of vitamin	Sources	Functions	Effects of too little	Notes
Vitamin A 1 Retinol	■ Animal fats ■ Dairy foods ■ Fortified margarine ■ Eggs ■ Liver ■ Oily fish ■ Fish liver oils	■ Promotes healthy skin, hair, nails, respiratory tract ■ Aids good vision in dim light ■ Promotes growth	■ Poor resistance to infection (especially skin and chest) ■ Poor night vision ■ Blindness (if extreme deficiency) ■ Delayed growth	■ Fat-soluble ■ Excess vitamin A intake during pregnancy may harm baby. Pregnant women advised not to eat liver because of its high vitamin A content, nor to take vitamin A supplement
2 Carotene (orange/yellow pigment)	■ Green leafy vegetables ■ Carrots ■ Tomatoes ■ Apricots ■ Mangoes ■ Peaches			

B-group
B_1 Thiamin
B_2 Riboflavin
Niacin
B_6 Pyridoxine
B_{12} Cyanocobalamin
	■ Meat
	■ Liver
	■ Milk
	■ Green vegetables
	■ Pulses
	■ Whole grains
	■ Yeast
	■ Eggs
	■ Breakfast cereals
		■ Aids:
		  – healthy working of muscles and nerves
		  – conversion of carbohydrate to energy and iron to haemoglobin
		■ Promotes healthy teeth and gums
		■ Guards against anaemia
			■ Muscle wasting
			■ Digestive problems
			■ Loss of appetite
			■ Anaemia
			■ Deficiency disorders:
			  – Beri beri
			  – Pellagra
			  – Pernicious anaemia
				■ Water-soluble
				■ Tend to occur in same foods
				■ Easily destroyed in cooking
				■ Usually added to breakfast cereals

Folic acid/Folate	■ Liver ■ Potatoes ■ Green leafy vegetables ■ Bread ■ Fortified breakfast cereals	■ Guards against anaemia ■ Helps reduce risk of foetal neural tube defects	Linked to anencephaly and spina bifida in the newborn (failure of brain and spinal cord to develop properly)	■ Easily destroyed in cooking ■ Supplements recommended preconceptually and in early pregnancy

Table 2.1   Vitamins (continued)

Name of vitamin	Sources	Functions	Effects of too little	Notes

Vitamin C (Ascorbic acid)	■ Citrus fruits
	  – oranges
	  – lemons
	  – limes
	  – grapefruit
	■ Strawberries
	■ Blackcurrants
	■ Pure fruit juices
	■ Sweet peppers
	■ Guavas
	■ Potatoes, sweet potatoes
	■ Tomatoes
	■ Green leafy vegetables
		■ Promotes:
		  – healthy skin
		  – healing
		■ Aids:
		  – absorption of iron
		  – teeth and bone formation
		■ Builds strong body tissues and blood vessels
			■ Poor resistance to infection
			■ Delayed healing
			■ Anaemia
			■ Scurvy
				■ Water-soluble
				■ Easily destroyed in cooking and keeping food hot
				■ The content of vitamin C in fruit and vegetables varies according to season, freshness and variety

Vitamin D (Calciferol) 'sunshine vitamin'	■ Fish liver oils
	■ Oily fish
	■ Butter
	■ Eggs
	■ Fortified foods
	  – margarine
	  – infant formula
	■ Milk and cheese (small amount)
	■ Sunlight
		■ Necessary for:
		■ bone and teeth formation
		■ absorption of calcium and phosphorus
			■ Dental caries
			■ Rickets
				■ Fat-soluble
				■ Can be made in the body (synthesised) by action of sunlight on skin

Vitamin E (Tocopherol)	■ Eggs
	■ Soya products
	■ Wheat germ
	■ Vegetable oils
	■ Green vegetables
	■ Nuts and seeds
		■ Aids:
		  – blood clotting
		  – fat metabolism
		  – production of male and female sex hormones
		■ Promotes healing
			■ Heart and blood disorders
			■ Muscle and tissue damage
			■ May contribute to miscarriages
				■ Fat-soluble, but cannot be stored for long

Vitamin K	■ Green vegetables ■ Alfalfa ■ Soya bean ■ Wholegrains ■ Egg yolk ■ Liver	■ Needed for: ■ clotting of blood ■ wound healing	■ Excessive bleeding ■ Delayed healing	■ Fat-soluble ■ Can be made from bacteria in the intestine ■ Given routinely in some instances to infants at birth

Table 2.2 Minerals

Major mineral	Sources	Functions	Effects of too little	Notes
Iron	■ Meat, liver, kidney ■ Egg yolk ■ Oily fish ■ Green leafy vegetables ■ Wholemeal bread ■ Fortified white breads and breakfast cereals ■ Pulses ■ Dried fruits – apricots – prunes – raisins and sultanas ■ Cocoa	■ Forms haemoglobin, which carries oxygen to all body tissues	Iron-deficiency anaemia: ■ lack of energy ■ breathlessness ■ pallor ■ infections ■ delayed growth	■ Vitamin C aids absorption so green vegetables, salads, potatoes, fresh fruit at mealtimes are important ■ Tannin in tea inhibits iron absorption ■ Iron especially important: – in childhood and adolescence – during pregnancy and lactation
Calcium	■ Dairy foods ■ Pulses ■ Fish and fish bones (sardines, pilchards salmon) ■ Watercress and other green leafy vegetables ■ Fortified flours and breads ■ Hard water	■ Maintains strong bones and teeth ■ Aids: – normal muscle function – blood clotting	■ Dental caries ■ Rickets (bones fail to harden) ■ Muscle cramps ■ Delayed blood clotting	■ Vitamin D aids absorption ■ Calcium not well absorbed by body and children unable to eat dairy products should be carefully monitored
Phosphorus	■ Dairy foods ■ Meat ■ Fish ■ Eggs ■ Cereals ■ Fruit and vegetables and most other foods	■ Combines with calcium for strong bones and teeth ■ Aids absorption of carbohydrate ■ Helps to maintain fluid balance in body	■ Deficiency rare but can occur in kidney disease	■ High intake in first few days of life from using unmodified cow's milk may result in tetany (muscle spasms)

Table 2.2 Minerals (*continued*)

Major mineral	Sources	Functions	Effects of too little	Notes
Sodium chloride (salt)	■ Common salt ■ Fresh meat and fish ■ Processed foods ■ Cured bacon and ham ■ Smoked fish (kippers) ■ Crisps (salted)	■ Maintains fluid balance in body ■ Aids transmission of nerve impulses ■ Assists muscle activity	■ Muscle cramps ■ Tiredness	■ A high intake of salt is linked to high blood pressure ■ Salt should not be added to foods for babies and young children
Potassium	■ Meat ■ Milk ■ Wholegrain cereals/foods ■ Fruit ■ Vegetables ■ Coffee	■ Works closely with sodium in maintaining fluid balance	■ Dietary deficiency rare	■ Widely distributed in fresh foods ■ Coffee unsuitable for young children
Trace elements				
Fluoride	■ Fluoridated water ■ Bones of fish (sardines, pilchards, salmon) ■ Fluoride tablets or drops ■ Toothpaste	■ Makes tooth enamel more resistant to decay	■ Dental caries	■ Too much fluoride can cause mottling of teeth and delay shedding ■ Fluoridation of water supplies is a controversial policy

The food groups

Foods are usually grouped according to the *main nutrient*, or *nutrients* they supply. Putting food into groups makes it easier to plan meals and snacks. Five **food groups** are identified in the text and diagram below. As you work your way through the groups, refer to the nutrient charts and tables on pages 17–27.

The five food groups

Group One – Starchy carbohydrates: breads, cereals, rice and pasta, semolina and sago, also starchy vegetables, such as potatoes, sweet potatoes, cassava, yams, plantain. All these foods are important high-calorie carbohydrate foods which provide children with energy for warmth, growth and physical activities, such as running, climbing, skipping, PE, swimming, etc.

They should form a substantial part of every child's diet (see the diagrams on Cereals and grains and Vegetables, pages 13 and 15).

Group Two – Fruit and vegetables: the abundant varieties of available fruit and vegetables are rich in vitamins and minerals, and many are a good source of natural sugar and fibre. They promote general good health and protect against infection and specific disorders (see Iron-deficiency anaemia, Chapter 8, pages 128–30 and Vitamin deficiency disorders, pages 134–5).

Group Three – Milk and **dairy foods**: milk, butter, cheese, cream, yoghurt and fromage frais are rich in calcium, protein and fat. They are important for growth, energy, general good health, and strong, healthy bones and teeth. (See Milk, Chapter 3, pages 37–8, for the importance of milk in children's nutrition and also the fat content of milk.)

Group Four – Meat, poultry, fish and alternatives: meat includes red and white meat and offal (liver, hearts and kidneys). Poultry includes chicken and turkey, duck and goose. Alternatives refer to vegetable and plant products, such as pulses, quorn, textured vegetable protein (TVP) and tofu. All these are protein foods needed for growth and for healing, repair and maintenance of body tissues. Oily fish, such as mackerel, tuna, herring and sardines, contain essential fatty acids, which promote healthy brain function. Quorn (a mycoprotein) is a mushroom-type fungus eaten instead of meat, TVP is a vegetable-based (often soya bean) meat substitiute and tofu is textured soya bean curd (see Proteins chart, page 17).

Group Five – Fatty foods and sugary foods: foods in this group are high in calories and may contain little else of nutrient value. They include fat spreads; sugar, sugary drinks, ice-cream, chocolate, sweets; biscuits, cakes, pastries, powdered desserts, pies (especially bought ones) and crisps. Foods in this group should provide only a *small* fraction of calorie intake (see Occasional foods, Chapter 3, pages 46–8).

Study the food groups. As you work your way through them check with the nutrient charts on pages 17–27. In Chapter 3 you will see how to include foods from these groups in children's diets.

REMEMBER!

There are nutrients other than 'main' nutrients in many foods. For example, breads and other starchy foods provide B-group vitamins and fibre as well as energy; milk (the most complete food of all) contains carbohydrate, **lactose** (milk sugar), vitamins, minerals and water in addition to calcium, protein and fat; and red meat, rich in protein, also contains fat and iron.

Dairy, staple and fortified foods

DAIRY FOODS

Dairy foods, also known as milk foods, include milk, butter, cheese, yoghurt and fromage frais.

STAPLE FOODS

Staple foods are foods that are commonly eaten and form the bulk of a diet. Examples are bread and potatoes in Northern Europe, rice in Far Eastern countries and millet (mealie) in Africa.

FORTIFIED FOODS

Fortified foods are those that have vitamins and/or minerals added to them. Some foods are fortified by law. These are:

■ margarine, which has vitamins A and D added
■ white flour (and products made from it), which has iron, calcium, vitamin B_1 (Thiamin) and Niacin added.

This helps to ensure that children whose overall diet may be generally poor do not suffer from vitamin or mineral deficiency.

QUICK CHECK

1 Name the seven essential nutrients.
2 Explain the importance in the diet of:
  (a) protein
  (b) carbohydrate
  (c) iron.
3 What do you understand by the terms 'high biological value' protein and 'low biological value' protein?
4 What is protein complementation?
5 Name the two minerals needed for the formation of bones and teeth.
6 Name the vitamins necessary for the absorption of:
  (a) calcium
  (b) iron.
7 Describe the terms:
  (a) fat-soluble
  (b) water-soluble.
8 Name the fat-soluble and water-soluble vitamins.
9 Name the principal nutrients in the following foods:
  (a) white fish
  (b) red meat
  (c) lentils
  (d) milk
  (e) cheese
  (f) wholegrain bread
  (g) pasta and rice
  (h) plantain
  (i) carrots
  (j) broccoli
  (k) tomatoes
  (l) oranges
  (m) strawberries
  (n) cream
  (o) butter
  (p) fortified margarine
  (q) peanuts.
10 How many food groups are there?
11 Name the foods in each of the food groups.
12 Which foods are known as 'dairy foods'?
13 What are the staple foods of Northern Europe and Africa?
14 What do you understand by the term 'fortified foods'?
15 Why are some foods fortified?

KEY WORDS AND TERMS

You need to know what these words and phrases mean. Go back through the chapter and find out.

amino acids

animal protein

dairy foods

food groups

fortified foods

high and low biological value

protein complementation

saturated and polyunsaturated fat

staple foods

unavailable carbohydrate

vegetable protein

3 BALANCED NUTRITION

> ## This chapter covers:
> ■ **Well-balanced nutrition for children**
> ■ **The principles of nutrition for children**
> ■ **Daily portion intakes**
> ■ **Healthy snacks**
> ■ **Planning balanced menus**
> ■ **Nutritional needs in adolescence, before conception and in pregnancy**

Common health problems among the adult population in the UK include the following:

■ obesity
■ dental disease
■ high blood pressure
■ coronary heart disease
■ arthritis
■ diabetes (late onset)
■ varicose veins
■ constipation
■ haemorrhoids
■ large bowel disorders.

Although changing lifestyles, smoking and lack of exercise may contribute to some of these problems, incorrect or poor diet is a major factor. Even very young children suffer from obesity, dental disease and constipation. Parents and Early Years workers have a responsibility to provide nutritious meals and snacks for children, help them to establish healthy attitudes to food and set good eating patterns. This will reduce the risk of diet-related problems both in childhood and adult life. Try and set an example for children by eating and enjoying healthy foods yourself. Involve children in menu planning, buying and preparing food to encourage them to take an interest in what they are eating and increase their knowledge of different foods. Children should never be 'put on a diet' by parents or carers. For different reasons some children may need to follow a diet prescribed by the doctor or nutritionist.

Well-balanced nutrition for children

During the first year of life physical growth is rapid. Growth then continues at a slower, steadier rate. Relative to their size children have high energy and nutritional needs. Because they eat smaller portions of food than adults, the food offered must be *'energy and nutrient dense'*.

Well-balanced nutrition for children means offering them a *wide variety* of foods. This will ensure they receive all the energy, essential nutrients and nourishment to grow and remain healthy. By eating a *variety* of food there will be less chance of nutrient deficiency. If a particular nutrient is not in one food it will be in another. A varied diet, which may include foods from different cultures, will also offer children interesting alternatives at mealtimes.

Children's nutrition should be built around the following *four* groups from the five food groups described in Chapter 2, pages 28–9:

■ starchy carbohydrates (including wholegrains)
■ fruit and vegetables
■ lean meat, poultry, fish and/or vegetable and plant alternatives
■ milk and dairy foods.

Children must also be offered adequate water to drink.

Foods from food group five (fatty foods and sugary foods) can be offered occasionally. However, children whose nutritional intake includes a high proportion of foods rich in fat and sugar and few other nutrients will be at risk from diet-related disorders. On the whole, children eat too many very fatty, sugary foods, too much salt and too many additives.

Dinner time in the nursery

Children need at least three small, nutrient-dense meals every day, plus two or three healthy snacks. Very young children may require more frequent meals. Meals and snacks for children should be inviting and stimulating to the taste and varied in texture. They should be served calmly and quietly and the children allowed adequate time to eat them (see Mealtimes for children, Chapter 5, pages 81-4.)

You can check whether a child's diet is adequate by assessing:
- the child's state of health
- the child's growth and development pattern
- the child's energy output.

It may sometimes be necessary to assess the nutrient content of a child's diet. This should be carried out over a period of two to three weeks and not made on one day's nutritional intake.

The chart below outlines how balanced nutrition promotes health and development in children.

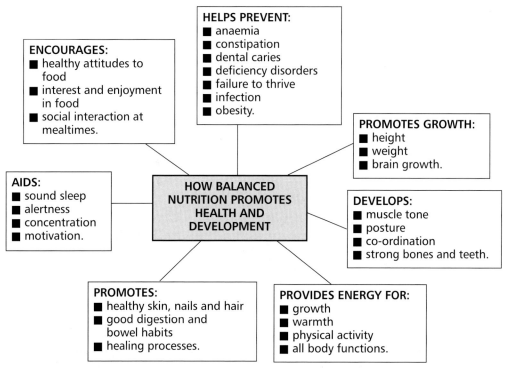

How balanced nutrition promotes health and development

The principles of nutrition for children

PROTEIN AND ENERGY

The first nutritional requirements for children are for protein and energy.

Protein

The need for protein is great during the periods of rapid growth in infancy and adolescence, and also during the steady growth in childhood years. It is also needed at times of injury, illness and infection.

Too little protein in early life, when the brain is developing rapidly, may result in learning delay as well as poor weight and height growth. Children may, for reasons of culture, religion or parental preference, be offered vegetable and plant, rather than animal, sources of protein, so a *wide variety and mixture* of pulses and cereal foods will be needed to ensure they receive all the amino acids necessary for growth.

Using up energy in the playground

Energy

Children need energy for growth and to replace energy used up in their busy, active day. Their calorie requirement is high and should be supplied by the following:

■ Starchy carbohydrate foods – a variety of breads, cereals, pasta and rice (wholegrains as well as white varieties), also vegetables such as potatoes, sweet potatoes, cassava, plantain and yams (see Chapter 2, pages 13–15, 19).

■ Fats and oils – these are an important source of energy for young children. However, they are a *concentrated* form of energy providing twice the number of calories per gram as carbohydrates. Saturated fat is particularly found in dairy products and lean meat – foods that also provide important protein, fat-soluble vitamins and other nutrients, in addition to energy. It is good dietary practice to offer children sensible, regular amounts of these foods, including a pint of milk every day (see below). Polyunsaturated fats, found in oily fish (mackerel, salmon, tuna, sardines and herrings), and in corn and sunflower oils and soya products, contain essential fatty acids (EFAs), which are very beneficial to a child's health. Butter and vegetable spreads, including margarine, can be used on bread and toast or as a topping for potatoes and vegetables.

REMEMBER!

■ **There is no substitute for protein**. If energy requirements are not met by carbohydrates and fats, protein will be used instead to supply essential energy rather than being used to promote growth.
■ Low-fat diets, often recommended for adults, are unsuitable for children.

MILK

Whole (full-fat) milk is one of the most complete foods available and plays an important part in a healthy diet for children, especially those whose diet may be generally poor. It is a rich source of protein and fat, calcium and phosphorus, vitamin A and the B-group vitamins. It also contains some vitamin C and vitamin D. The content of vitamins A, B_2 (Riboflavin) and C are reduced if the milk is exposed to sunlight, for example if it is left on a doorstep for some time.

The Department of Health recommends 1 pint of weaned milk daily for children under 5 years, especially for its fat (energy) content and vitamins A and D. The Food Standards Agency advises that children can be given semi-skimmed milk from the age of 2 years, as long as they are eating a varied and balanced diet. Skimmed milk is not suitable for children under 5 years as it limits their intake of fat and affects their calorie and fat-soluble vitamin intake. Children may be offered milk in a variety of ways – as a drink, in puddings, custard and sauces, with cereals or as cheese or plain yoghurt.

The energy, protein and fat content of milks is as follows:
■ One pint of whole milk provides:
1610 kJ/387 kcal
19 g protein
23 g fat.

- One pint of semi-skimmed milk provides:
  1145 kJ/270 kcal
  19.4 g protein
  9.4 g fat.
- One pint of skimmed milk provides:
  824 kJ/194 kcal
  19.4 g protein
  0.6 g fat.

REMEMBER!

Whole, semi-skimmed and skimmed milks are all good sources of calcium and phosphorus.

SUGAR

Sugar provides nothing but **'empty' calories**. It is not necessary as a source of energy – starchy carbohydrates, fats and other nutrients will provide all the energy a child needs. Many foods such as milk, fruit and vegetables contain natural sugar, but these foods also provide other essential nutrients such as vitamins, minerals and fibre.

On the whole, natural sugars make up only a small proportion of the total sugar eaten. It is the refined sugars *added* to foods and drinks that constitute a threat to health. These include white and brown table sugars, which provide about 20 kcal per average teaspoon.

Sugar should not be added to children's food and drinks. Pure fruit juice or fresh or dried fruits can be used in baking, and as pudding and cereal sweeteners. A variety of fruits can be added to plain yoghurt. Try using flour or oatmeal mixed with sunflower oil as a topping for fruit crumble instead of the traditional sugar, butter and flour mixture. Rice pudding can be made with brown rice and sweetened with dates, raisins or sultanas. Offer children low-sugar cereals and sugar-free or low-sugar jams. Jellies can be home-made using gelatine and unsweetened fruit juice. Limit sweets and chocolate, if given, to once or twice a week. Naturally sweet-tasting vegetables such as carrots, celery, sweetcorn and sweet peppers are appetising and nutritious.

SALT

High salt (sodium) intake in childhood is linked to high blood pressure in later life. In turn, raised blood pressure increases the risk of coronary heart disease, stroke and kidney disease.

The immature kidneys of an infant are unable to cope with salt, but after the age of 1 year there is less risk of kidney damage. However, salt is not needed when preparing and cooking food for children and the use of table salt should be discouraged. The amount of salt occurring naturally in many foods is sufficient for the body's needs and it is better for children's health if they do not develop a taste for salty foods. Fresh herbs will enhance the flavour of foods if necessary. Most processed foods contain salt. Read the labels of processed foods, looking for words such as salt, soy or sodium (glutamate, bicarbonate, nitrate or nitrite; see Chapter 9).

FIBRE

A high-fibre diet, which might be recommended for an adult, is unsuitable for children as it fills them up, leaving little room for essential nutrients, and may cause stomach pains. Fibre in the form of raw bran can prevent the absorption of important minerals such as calcium and zinc and should not be given to children.

Offering children wholegrain cereals, bread, pasta and rice (including brown rice pudding), as well as fruit (fresh and dried), assorted raw and cooked vegetables and jacket potatoes will provide them with adequate fibre. Pulses are a good source of fibre and can be used in casseroles, soups, flans, salads and burgers. Red kidney beans are used in chilli con carne, dahl is made from lentils and hummus is made with chick peas. Wholemeal flour can be used for baking. All these foods will encourage chewing, promote healthy bowel habits and reduce the risk of constipation.

WATER AND OTHER DRINKS

Milk, water and occasional drinks of diluted, unsweetened pure fruit juice should provide an adequate fluid intake for children. Offer them regular drinks of fresh tap water at and between mealtimes, especially in hot weather or whenever they are thirsty. Babies under 1 year can have cooled, boiled water. Tea and coffee are not advised as drinks for young children. They both contain the stimulant caffeine, while tea contains tannin, which inhibits the absorption of iron. Of course, sugar added to tea or coffee can affect dental health and contribute to overweight.

The minerals sodium (salt) and potassium, plus good kidney function, play a vital role in maintaining the fluid balance in the body – too much or too little of either mineral can affect health, as can a variety of kidney disorders. Natural mineral waters are unsuitable for young children as their sodium content may overload their kidneys, and if the fluoride level is high, there is danger of damage to tooth enamel.

Providing children with a sensible range of food and adequate drinks will keep their sodium, potassium and water levels in balance and prevent thirst.

REMEMBER!

Dehydration (loss of water from the body) can be caused by:
■ diarrhoea and vomiting
■ high temperature
■ mouth and throat infections, which make drinking and swallowing painful
■ diabetes
■ insufficient fluid intake, especially during hot weather.
These conditions can be serious and you should always seek advice if you are concerned about dehydration in a baby or young child.

FRUIT AND VEGETABLES

Fruit and vegetables are excellent sources of vitamins, minerals and fibre, and many contain a lot of water. Children should be encouraged to eat fruit and/or vegetables at every meal and snack time. Cooking and processing can destroy much of the vitamin and mineral content, so offer children a variety of fresh and dried fruits and pieces of raw or lightly cooked vegetables to retain these nutrients. Fruits can be offered as freshly squeezed juice, used in fruit salads, crumbles, tarts and sponge puddings or eaten as individual portions. They can also be added to yoghurt and milk shakes. Children enjoy tropical fruits such as guavas, mangoes and papayas, also kiwi fruit, as well as the more familiar fruits they regularly eat. Vegetable juices and soups, casseroles and quiches, salads (lettuce, cucumber, tomatoes, grated carrot or cabbage, sweet peppers) and salad sandwiches are all good ways to incorporate vegetables into children's diets.

Activity
1. (a) Write down the number of servings of fruit and vegetables the children in your setting are offered over a five-day period. Remember to include those offered at 'snack' breaks.
   (b) In how many different ways were the fruits and vegetables incorporated into the children's daily meals and snacks? Examples are raw, cooked, grated, in flans, casseroles, yoghurt, etc.
2. Find out how you would prepare guavas, mangoes and papayas ready for children to eat.

NUTS AND SEEDS

Nuts and seeds provide many valuable nutrients, including EFAs. Whole or broken nuts and seeds are unsuitable for young children under 5 years of age because of the danger of choking. Ground nuts and seeds can be used in baking, cooking or spreads. Peanut butter and tahini spreads make nutritious fillings for sandwiches.

However, nut allergy (especially allergy to peanuts) is always a possibility. If a close member of a child's family has any allergy, asthma or hayfever (known as being 'atopic'), it is advised that the child should not eat nuts until the age of 3. This may have a preventative effect. The eventual introduction of nuts should be gradual and controlled, and the child should be observed for any adverse affects.

Because of the risk of allergies, most early years settings have introduced a 'no nut' policy. They do not use nuts or nut products, and children are not permitted to bring them into the setting.

In summary, always remember to check with carers before offering foods such as nut spread, or cheesecake or flan with a nut base, to any child. A severe reaction to nuts can be very serious, even life-threatening (for more on allergies, see Chapter 6, pages 102–7).

DIETARY SUPPLEMENTS

Daily supplements of vitamins A, D and C, available from the Child Health Clinic, are recommended for children under 5 years.

Children under 5 years of age whose parents receive income support are entitled to free vitamins. Child Health Clinics are part of the Community Child Health Service. They offer a range of provision for well babies and young children, including immunisation, health and development check-ups and screening tests for vision and hearing.

Should these be on the nursery or school meal table?

REMEMBER!

■ Children need high protein and high energy nutrition.
■ Whole milk must be given to weaned children up to the age of 2.
■ From 2 years, semi-skimmed milk may be given.

- Skimmed milk must not be given until children are 5 years of age.
- Offer foods that are low in salt and sugar. Do not add salt or sugar.
- Provide fibre in the form of wholegrains, fruit (fresh and dried) and raw and cooked vegetables. No raw bran.
- Offer children milk or fresh water to drink.
- Extra fluid is necessary in hot weather.
- Do not offer whole or broken nuts and seeds to children under 5 years (don't forget the possibility of nut allergy).
- Vitamin supplements are recommended up to 5 years.

Daily portion intakes

Children's appetites and nutritional needs vary according their age, size and energy levels. Toddlers often go through phases of food refusal and foods fads as they strive to be independent. Many 3–4 year olds are unpredictable in their eating patterns, eating little one day and everything the next. Some 7–8 year olds have big appetites, eating almost adult-sized meals. Children will neither starve themselves nor eat to excess (except, perhaps, at parties). They usually know when they are sufficiently full and when they have 'room for seconds'.

By following the recommended daily portion intakes for children set out below, Early Years workers will ensure adequate nutritional intake for children in their care.

Recommended daily portion intakes for children are:

- Food Group One (energy-rich, starchy carbohydrate foods): *five* portions
- Food Group Two (fruit and vegetables): *five* portions
- Food Group Three (milk and dairy foods): *four* portions
- Food Group Four (meat, poultry, fish and alternatives): *two* portions
- Food Group Five (fatty foods and sugary foods) (see Chapter 2, page 29): *no recommended daily portions*; can be offered occasionally

plus

- approximately 1½ pints (1 litre) of fluids, of which 1 pint (500–600 ml) will be milk.

For more on the five food groups, see Chapter 2, pages 28–9.

REMEMBER!

Potatoes are not included in the fruit and vegetable portions. They are a starchy food and come under carbohydrates in Food Group One.

SOME TYPICAL AVERAGE PORTIONS

Examples of one *average* portion are:
  (tbsp = tablespoon 1 oz = 28 g)
■ *Starchy carbohydrate foods*:
  Bread: one medium slice or ½ large slice
  Rolls: one medium or ½ a burger bun
  Cereals: cornflakes, rice crispies, 3–4 tbsp; Weetabix or similar, 1 biscuit
  Cooked rice and pasta: 2 tbsp
  Potatoes: 1 medium boiled or 2 tbsp mashed
■ *Fruit and vegetables*:
  Fruit: 1 small or ½ large apple, banana, orange or pear; 6 stoned cherries or small bunch of grapes (halved and pips removed); drink of juice (fruit/vegetable) in beaker, 168 ml/6 oz; dried fruit (raisins, sultanas, apricots, etc.), 1 tbsp
  Vegetables: for example, cooked carrots, peas and sweetcorn 2 tbsp, a few sticks of raw carrot, celery or similar
■ *Milk and dairy foods*:
  Whole milk drink (or milk shake made from whole milk) in a beaker, 168 ml/6 oz
  Hard cheese (cheddar, gruyère, parmesan): 28 g/1 oz slice, or 1 tbsp grated
  Yoghurt: 1 pot
■ *Meat, poultry, fish or alternatives*:
  Meat and poultry: 1 medium slice cooked
  Cooked, minced meat: 2 tbsp
  Bacon: 1 slice
  Sausage: 1 medium
  Egg: 1 medium
  White fish (baked or steamed): 56 g/2 oz
  Well-cooked pulses, baked beans: 2 tbsp

REMEMBER!

■ Toddlers will need smaller portions of some foods. As long as they have a variety of foods from the four groups every day, including a pint of milk or the equivalent in dairy products, they will receive all the nutrients they need.
■ Eggs must be well cooked to reduce the risk of salmonella infection. Eggs can be boiled, scrambled or poached, or cooked in egg custard or cakes (see Key Points, Chapter 4, page 73).

Table 3.1 The nutritional value of foods, per 100 g (3½ oz)

Food	Energy kJ	kcal	Protein g	Fat g	Calcium mg	Iron mg	Vitamin A µg	Vitamin C µg
Cheddar cheese	1708	412	26	34	720	0.3	363	0
Cottage cheese	413	98	13.6	4	73	0.1	46	0
Bread (white)	1002	235	8.4	2	110	1.6	0	0
Bread (wholemeal)	914	215	9.2	2.5	54	2.7	0	0
Apple	196	46	0.3	0	4	0.3	5	5
Orange	150	35	0.8	0	41	0.3	8	50
Weetabix								
Baked beans								
Chocolate biscuits								
Butter								
Plain yoghurt								
Rice								

Healthy snacks

Children need two to three healthy snacks a day. They are important in the overall dietary provision for young children, complementing main meals. Snack foods can be interesting, imaginative and colourful, and should reflect different cultural tastes. Some examples are:

■ pieces of fresh or dried fruits (dried fruits, such as apricots, apples, stoned dates and prunes, pineapple and figs, as well as sultanas, currants and raisins, are good sources of minerals and fibre.)
■ diluted, unsweetened pure fruit juice or a milk drink and plain biscuit
■ sandwiches using assorted breads and rolls (including wholegrain) with fillings, such as cottage or hard cheese, chicken, ham, tuna, yeast extract, peanut butter, salad ingredients, tahini, hummus or banana
■ washed raw vegetables, such as carrots, celery and white cabbage cut into manageable pieces
■ plain yoghurt flavoured with chopped fresh fruit
■ milk shake (whole milk flavoured with liquidised fresh fruit).

SAFE PRACTICE

■ Use ground nuts, not whole or broken ones, when cooking for children under 5 years.
■ Check with carers for nut or other food allergy.
■ Comply with any 'no nut' policies in settings.
■ To prevent choking episodes in young children:

- Supervise them carefully when they are eating pieces of hard foods such as carrot, celery, cabbage, apples. Carrots and apples can be grated or partially cooked.
- Fruits must be washed and peeled (if necessary). Cut them into manageable pieces according to a child's ability to bite, chew and swallow. Remove all pips, seeds, and stones from fruits such as nectarines, peaches, plums and papayas. Oranges, mandarins, satsumas and tangerines may need the membrane removed from the segments as well as the pips. Grapes should be halved and the pips removed.
- ■ Older children (5–7 years) will manage a range of fruits such as apples, oranges, bananas, peaches, nectarines and plums. However, make sure they can take care of the stones and pips.
- ■ Children should sit down to eat meals and snacks. Walking or running around when eating or drinking can contribute to accidents, including choking.
- ■ Always offer children their drinks in plastic or polythene beakers, not glasses. Milk provided in schools will be in cartons.

Activity
Think of a variety of ways to provide (a) potatoes and (b) cheddar cheese for children as part of their overall balanced nutrition.

OCCASIONAL FOODS

Occasional foods are those referred to in Food Group Five. There is a whole range of energy-dense, fatty, sugary foods available, many of which form a large part of some children's diets either as meals or snacks, and contribute to obesity, iron deficiency anaemia and dental caries. Deep-fried and battered foods (chips, burgers and fish, etc.) are saturated with fat or oil, greatly increasing calorie intake. Bought pies, pasties, sausages and sausage rolls are high in fat, as is mayonnaise, a favourite addition to salads and sandwiches. Crisps can be high in fat and salt. Bought cakes, buns, pastries and sweet biscuits (especially chocolate varieties and those with marshmallow or icing), sweets, chews and chocolate, fruit squashes, fizzy drinks and jellies, sugary cereals, ice-cream, powdered milk drinks and desserts are all sugar-rich foods. Processed foods, such as baked beans, bottled sauces, pickles and salad dressings are usually high in added sugars – although low-sugar and low-salt baked beans are available.

All the above foods are firm favourites with many children and cannot be totally excluded from their diets. However, they should only be offered

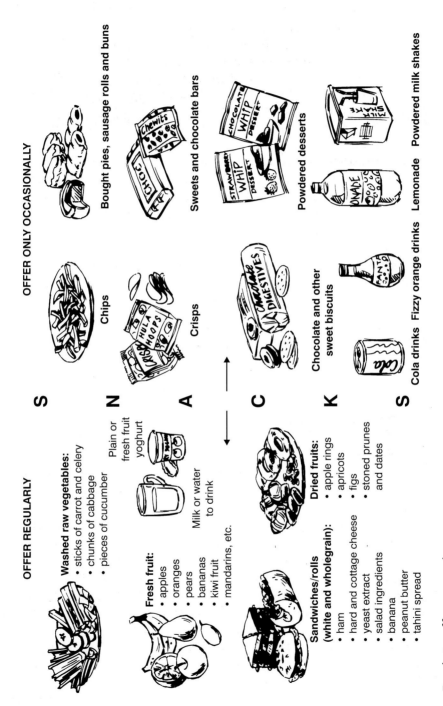

S

Washed raw vegetables:
• sticks of carrot and celery
• chunks of cabbage
• pieces of cucumber

Plain or fresh fruit yoghurt

Chips

N

Fresh fruit:
• apples
• oranges
• pears
• bananas
• kiwi fruit
• mandarins, etc.

Milk or water to drink

Crisps

A

Sandwiches/rolls (white and wholegrain):
• ham
• hard and cottage cheese
• yeast extract
• salad ingredients
• banana
• peanut butter
• tahini spread

Dried fruits:
• apple rings
• apricots
• figs
• stoned prunes and dates

Bought pies, sausage rolls and buns

C

Sweets and chocolate bars

Chocolate and other sweet biscuits

K

Powdered desserts

S

Cola drinks   Fizzy orange drinks   Lemonade   Powdered milk shakes

Foods to offer as snacks

to children occasionally and form just a small fraction of their overall diet and energy intake.

Generally, home-made foods are fresher and healthier than processed ones with fewer artificial additives. Pies and burgers can be made from lean meat. Soups and casseroles, using a range of fresh vegetables and pulses (with or without meat or alternatives), are tasty and nutritious. Grilling, baking, steaming and poaching are healthier cooking methods than frying and roasting. Chips are less fatty when thickly sliced, fried in polyunsaturated fat and drained on kitchen paper.

REMEMBER!

■ Too many 'occasional foods' will leave a child with little room for the essential nutrient-rich foods and weaken the overall quality of their nutrition.
■ Check the nutritional labels on foods for fat, sugar, dextrose or glucose content. For more on Food labelling, see Chapter 9, page 153.

Planning balanced menus

When planning balanced menus for children you need to remember which foods will supply the essential nutrients, how much food they need and what religious, cultural or other dietary needs they may have. This will mean talking to parents and carers to find out about dietary habits and likes and dislikes.

You now have the theory for planning children's meals and snacks with five sources of knowledge to help you:
■ Dietary Reference Values (Chapter 1)
■ essential nutrients and food groups (Chapter 2)
■ principles of nutrition for children (Chapter 3)
■ daily portion intakes (Chapter 3)
■ snacks – their importance and examples (Chapter 3).

Activity
Would you change any of the following meals or snacks for children? Give reasons for both 'yes' and 'no' answers.
  1 Cornflakes, skimmed milk and sugar, drink of sweet tea.
  2 Fried bacon, sausage and chips, baked beans, tomato sauce, white bread and butter, drink of milk.

3 Home-made cheese and onion flan, baked potato, green salad and tomatoes, followed by fresh fruit salad and drink of water.
4 Wholewheat cracker spread lightly with butter, cheddar cheese and drink of milk.
5 Bought white burger bun filled with fried beef burger and onions, followed by a sticky bun, packet of crisps and can of cola.
6 Chicken curry, brown rice and poppadom, followed by jelly and ice-cream, drink of water.
7 Warm chocolate milk drink and plain biscuit.
8 Bought meat pie, tinned carrots, mashed potatoes, followed by tinned rice pudding and jam, fizzy orange drink.
9 Home-made cottage pie and peas, followed by stewed apples and custard, drink of water.
10 Baked white fish (boned), broccoli and mashed potatoes with parsley sauce, followed by 'instant whip' dessert and drink of milk.
11 Spaghetti bolognese followed by syrup sponge pudding and chocolate sauce, can of cola.
12 Breakfast cereal and chopped dried fruit with milk, grilled sausage and slice of wholemeal bread, diluted, unsweetened fruit juice to drink.
13 Lentil and chickpea casserole, wholegrain rice and mixed frozen vegetables, followed by plain yoghurt with chopped fresh fruit and drink of water.
14 Drink of milk, packet of cheese and onion crisps and two custard cream biscuits.
15 Bowl of home-made vegetable soup, wholemeal roll and butter, fresh apple and milky unsweetened tea to drink.

Nutritional needs in adolescence, before conception and in pregnancy

ADOLESCENCE

Adolescents have particular nutritional needs because of their rapid growth and hormonal, social and psychological changes. As they become more independent, taking control of their lives and making their own choices, they are greatly influenced by the behaviour, lifestyle and preferences of their peer group. Imitating the food choices of peers is often preferable to following nutritional advice offered by parents, teachers, health professionals and the informed media. Many adolescents do not eat breakfast and may miss other meals – particular pressures or activities may be of greater priority than eating. Irregular eating patterns and poor nutrient intake within a culture of 'snacking' on high energy foods are common, making obesity and vitamin and mineral deficiency a possibility. However, some snacks will provide nutrients other than energy and will form an important part of their overall diet.

Adolescents may be embarrassed by, or obsessed with, their body weight and follow a strict dietary regime. They may eat only small amounts of low energy foods, inadequate for normal health and growth. Some, preoccupied with body image and the desire to remain slim, may develop anorexia nervosa, exerting strict control over what they eat, and often exercising excessively to keep their weight as low as possible. Others may develop bulimia nervosa in an effort to prevent weight gain. Typically, this follows a pattern of secret binge-eating followed by self-induced vomiting, laxative abuse and, frequently, self-harming behaviour. While these eating disorders tend to affect more girls than boys, the incidence of anorexia among adolescent males is rising. The average age for onset of anorexia and bulimia is mid-teens. Both disorders are potentially life threatening and young people with either condition need specialist assessment and help.

Adolescents require a diet high in energy, protein, vitamins and minerals (see Table 1.2, page 5 for calorie requirements). Essential foods include starchy carbohydrates, fruit and vegetables, dairy foods and lean meat (or alternatives). Iron requirements increase during adolescence due to the growth spurt and, additionally for girls, to compensate for menstrual blood loss. Iron deficiency anaemia is common in adolescent girls as they tend to dislike iron-rich foods such as red meat, so eating a variety of pulses, green vegetables and foods containing vitamin C (necessary for iron absorption) is essential. Calcium is important for the increased muscle and bone growth. Intake will be affected if milk and other dairy foods are reduced too much. If weight reduction is advised it should be achieved through careful attention to diet and taking regular physical activity. Important vitamins and minerals will be lost if the intake of starchy carbohydrates and fruit and vegetables is reduced rather than unhealthy, high calorie fatty, sugary foods. The charts and tables on pages 17–27 detail the sources of all essential nutrients.

BEFORE CONCEPTION

By eating a balanced diet before conception (preconceptually) a woman can ensure that:
■ essential nutrients are stored in her body ready for her planned baby
■ the foetus is not subject to nutritional imbalances during the first 12 weeks of pregnancy.
Folic acid (folate), a B-group vitamin, is crucial for making foetal cells and

A balanced diet – healthy mother, healthy baby

for the development of the brain and spinal cord. Because these latter two structures form early in pregnancy, insufficient folic acid may lead to neural tube defects such as anencephaly (a defect of the skull and brain) or spina bifida. All women, especially those who have previously given birth to a baby with either condition, need advice from their doctor or midwife about foods rich in folic acid (see Table 2.1, pages 24–5) and should take extra folic acid supplements preconceptuallly and during the first 12 weeks of pregnancy.

The basic principles of healthy eating before conception are:

■ Eat daily from Food Groups One to Four (see pages 28–9).
■ Eat fresh foods whenever possible.
■ Reduce intake of sugar and sugary foods to a mimimum.
■ Cut down on fatty foods – eat polyunsaturates rather than saturated fats.
■ Cut down on salty foods – a high intake of salt is linked to high blood pressure, which can cause problems in pregnancy.

PREGNANCY

During pregnancy a woman's nutritional intake must provide sufficient energy and nutrients for:

■ her own health needs
■ growth of breasts, uterus and placenta
■ growth, nourishment and health of her developing baby
■ labour and breast-feeding.

An unborn baby receives nutrition from its mother via the placenta (after-birth). If a mother's dietary intake lacks the essential nutrients, or if the placenta fails to function properly (perhaps due to maternal heart or kidney conditions or high blood pressure), then the baby is likely to be born 'small for gestational age' (SGA). Nutrition in foetal life, and infancy, directly affects long-term health and babies born SGA are at risk of heart and lung disease and strokes in adult life. Maternal and foetal nutrition may be linked to the differences in health status between mothers in the various social classes. Expectant mothers who are poorly nourished because they are financially and educationally disadvantaged may have SGA babies. It is important that they are offered nutritional advice by those who care for them antenatally.

Girls who become pregnant in their teens, especially if they are still growing and physically immature themselves, may be at particular nutritional risk. They have special dietary needs both from being a teenager and from being pregnant. If normal eating habits are generally poor, reserves of some nutrients such as iron may be low with increased risk of anaemia developing. Dietary advice from the doctor and midwife and folic acid supplements in the early weeks of pregnancy are essential. When a girl is unaware that she is pregnant, or wishes to keep her pregnancy private, her attendance at antenatal clinic may be infrequent or not at all and the opportunity for nutritional advice is lost.

Nutrition in pregnancy
Extra calories are needed daily during pregnancy. These will come partly from the mother's diet and partly from naturally conserved energy as she rests more during her pregnancy. Healthy nutrition in pregnancy includes:

■ an extra pint of milk daily, or yoghurt or cheese, to provide calcium for the baby's bones and teeth and to contribute to the need for extra calories
■ foods containing iron (see Table 2.2, pages 26–7) to guard against anaemia and meet the foetal need to store iron in the liver during the latter weeks of pregnancy. Iron deficiency anaemia during pregnancy can result in a low birthweight baby and the risk of anaemia in the first two years of life. It may also seriously affect a mother's health should she have a heavy blood loss during birth
■ foods rich in folic acid
■ a variety of fresh fruit and vegetables, wholegrain breads, pasta and rice to maintain good health and to prevent constipation (a common condition in pregnancy). Bran-enriched cereals and drinks of water will also help to prevent constipation
■ vitamins, iron and folic acid supplements as advised by the doctor. These are especially important for women on low incomes or income support, or those eating restrictive diets
■ no alcohol, or just an occasional drink (but no more than two units per week).

The risk of contracting the following infections during pregnancy can be reduced by taking certain dietary precautions:

- *Listeriosis*, a bacterial infection that can cause miscarriage, stillbirth or serious illness in the newborn. Avoid soft and blue-veined cheeses (Brie, Camembert and Stilton) and paté; heat ready-cooked meals until they are piping hot; and thoroughly wash fruit and vegetables, especially if they are to be eaten raw.

- *Toxoplasmosis*, a parasitic illness caught from contact with cat faeces, which may cause vision impairment and developmental delay in the baby. Avoid raw or undercooked meat, unpasteurised goat's milk or goat's cheese and unwashed fruit or vegetables; and keep away from garden soil fouled by cats and cat litter trays (or use gloves when cleaning them).

- *Salmonella* bacterial poisoning, which can be passed to the baby. Avoid raw eggs or foods containing raw or partially cooked eggs; thoroughly cook meat and poultry; and practise good hand-washing and kitchen hygiene.

Eating liver is not recommended during pregnancy because of its high vitamin A content. This may be linked to foetal abnormality.

Women eating **vegetarian** or **vegan** diets should follow the principles in Chapter 10 to ensure a balanced, nutritious diet preconceptually and antenatally. Dietary advice is always available from family doctors, dieticians, midwives or health visitors.

Activity
Make up a three-day menu of three meals a day for the following expectant mothers:
1 an Asian woman
2 a woman who eats a vegan diet.

QUICK CHECK

1 What are the first nutritional requirements when planning meals for children?
2 What do you understand by the phrase 'well-balanced nutrition'?
3 How does well-balanced nutrition promote the overall development of children?
4 Name the main nutrients in whole milk. Which of them are affected by exposure to sunlight?
5 Why is skimmed milk unsuitable for young children?

6 Which words on a nutritional label would alert you to the presence in that food of:
   (a) sugar?
   (b) salt?
7 The use of refined sugars in children's diets contributes to dental caries and obesity. What could you use as a substitute, if necessary, for sweetening foods such as breakfast cereals and puddings?
8 What are the dangers of added salt in the diets of babies and young children?
9 Why are high-fibre diets unsuitable for children?
10 Name some possible causes of dehydration in young children.
11 What factors might influence the choice of food in adolescence?
12 The lack of which vitamin is thought to be linked to spina bifida in the newborn?
13 Why are extra calories needed in pregnancy?
14 What is the importance of iron in the diet of an expectant mother?
15 Why is liver not recommended in the diet during pregnancy?

KEY WORDS AND TERMS

You need to know what these words and phrases mean. Go back through the chapter and find out.

daily portion intakes
dehydration
diet before conception and in
   pregnancy
empty calories

protein and energy needs
typical average portions
well-balanced nutrition
whole milk nutrient value

4 *INFANT FEEDING*

This chapter covers:
- ■ **Breast or bottle?**
- ■ **Breast-feeding**
- ■ **Bottle-feeding**
- ■ **Weaning**
- ■ **Possible feeding difficulties**

Breast or bottle?

The choice between bottle-feeding and breast-feeding is an important one for any would-be parent. It is a decision best made after careful consideration of all the health promotion information available. It is a decision for the parents, and not one for carers and health professionals, to make. Pressure should not be placed on parents to make any particular decision; such pressure may result in a mother feeling guilty, for example, because she has decided not to breast-feed. This guilt may affect some of the pleasure of the early days of parenthood.

The antenatal period is the ideal time to give information about different feeding methods, as both parents have time to consider all the facts. Research tells us that parents are especially responsive to health information at this time. Social factors will affect their choice, just as much as health factors.

Activity

1 What might influence parents' decisions between breast-feeding and bottle-feeding when considering lifestyle and finance:
   (a) Which is cheaper?
   (b) How much equipment will be needed for each method?
   (c) What is the cost of a tin of formula milk?
   (d) How many tins will be required for one year?
   (e) How many feeding bottles will be required?
   (f) What types and amounts of sterilising equipment will be required?

Breast-feeding

Breast-feeding is nature's 'designer food'. The milk is specific to each individual baby and, although much can be copied in formula milks, the most important parts cannot. It changes as the baby grows and the baby's needs alter.

The rate of a baby's growth is greatest in the first year of life, but especially in the first months – the baby will usually double in birthweight by the age of 5 to 6 months and treble it by 12 months. The largest area of growth in these months is the brain. It is, therefore, very important that a baby's nutritional needs are met fully to allow this important development take place.

Breast milk is a complete food for the first months of life and no supplements are required.

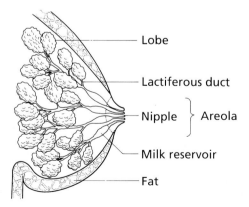

- Lobe
- Lactiferous duct
- Nipple } Areola
- Milk reservoir
- Fat

The lactating breast

HOW BREAST MILK IS MADE

The mature breast varies a great deal in size from one woman to another. The size of breast, nipple and areola (the dark area surrounding the nipple) are not related to the ability to produce milk successfully.

The important aspect of the nipple is its ability to become erect to allow the baby to become attached to (or to 'fix' at) the breast. The milk does not leave the breast through a single channel at the nipple, but through the lactiferous (milk-producing) ducts leading from each of the lobes (see the diagram opposite). (There are 15 to 20 ducts depending on the number of lobes or segments.) The areola also contains a number of small glands called Montgomery's tubercles, which become larger and more noticeable during pregnancy. They act like sweat glands and secrete a fluid that helps to keep the nipple soft and supple – a natural moisturing cream that should not be removed by washing with soap.

HOW THE MILK IS RELEASED

Breast milk is released by the **'let-down' reflex** (see the diagram below). Some women find this let-down sensation very strong, while others hardly notice it.

The breasts will only produce more milk when existing milk has been removed. Successful breast-feeding depends on 'supply and demand' – the more the baby feeds, the more milk is made. If this mechanism is broken, for example by giving the baby 'extra' in a bottle, future underproduction will result.

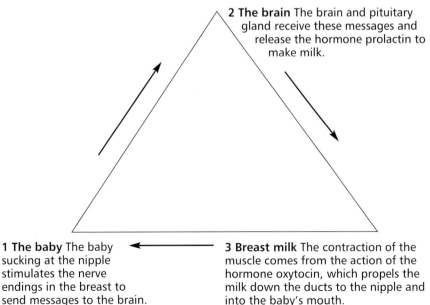

2 The brain The brain and pituitary gland receive these messages and release the hormone prolactin to make milk.

1 The baby The baby sucking at the nipple stimulates the nerve endings in the breast to send messages to the brain.

3 Breast milk The contraction of the muscle comes from the action of the hormone oxytocin, which propels the milk down the ducts to the nipple and into the baby's mouth.

The let-down reflex

THE COMPOSITION OF BREAST MILK

Breast milk is a changing food – it adapts to meet the needs of the growing baby.

Colostrum

This syrupy, yellowish substance is the important first milk made by the breasts from about the fifth month of pregnancy until about ten days after birth.

It protects the newborn baby from the more exposed and potentially dangerous environment outside the womb. It has a much higher protein content than later, mature breast milk and is low in fat and sugar. This is thought to be because:

■ the proteins contain many antibodies, which line the baby's intestines and prevent harmful bacteria entering the bloodstream
■ the high protein levels ensure that even the small amounts taken in will supply sufficient energy to allow the baby to sleep for long periods in the first days after birth.

For these reasons, even when not intending to continue, mothers are often actively encouraged to breast-feed for the first few days.

REMEMBER!

There is no artificial replacement for colostrum.

Mature breast milk

When milk begins to be made in the breasts and 'comes in' on the second to fourth day, it is still mixed with colostrum and looks rich and creamy. By the tenth day the mature milk looks thin and watery by comparison. The change in appearance does not reflect a change in composition, which is natural and appropriate to the baby's needs.

By the end of the fourth week, breast milk contains approximately a fifth of the protein of colostrum and more fat and glucose. The milk at the begining of a feed is called the '**fore milk**'. It is high in lactose (milk sugar) for a quick energy boost. With the let-down reflex comes the '**hind milk**', which has a higher fat content and so is rich in calories to meet the baby's growth needs. It also satisfies the baby for longer.

Human milk is almost completely digestible. The proteins are broken down into soft curds and quickly pass through into the small intestine. Water forms the liquid part of the milk.

All milks are poor sources of iron and a baby depends on the stores laid down in the liver during pregnancy. These supplies will last until the baby is 4–6 months old. Although breast milk is low in iron, the small amount present is absorbed well through the high concentration of lactose and vitamin C.

MANAGEMENT OF BREAST-FEEDING

A mother breast-feeding her baby will benefit from the support you can give her by explaining and answering her questions. She will be helped by understanding that it may take time for her and her baby to get to know each other and that, although breast-feeding is natural, many first-time mothers need additional support to establish feeding patterns.

It is thought to be important for the baby to be put to the breast as soon as possible after birth. This 'skin-to-skin' contact helps the mother and her baby to develop a loving relationship and, in addition, the sucking helps release hormones that contract the uterus back to its pre-pregnancy state.

The mother needs a comfortable position when feeding, for example, she may prefer to lie on her side if her perineum is sore. Pain can impair the let-down reflex and the flow of milk, so feeding in comfort is important. Chairs should give good support to the lower back, feet can be put on a stool if needed and privacy provided.

'Fixing' at the breast

The baby will use a rooting reflex to search for the breast. This can best be achieved by stimulating the baby's mouth with the mother's nipple. The baby will then turn to the breast and suck. Take the baby to the breast and never force the breast into the baby's mouth.

The baby is correctly fixed at the breast when the nipple and areola are in the baby's mouth. Sucking on the nipple alone will cause soreness. When successfully fixed, the baby's mouth will be wide open with the bottom lip curled back and some way from the base of the nipple (see the diagram on page 60). If the baby's nose is pressing into the breast and causing her to come off frequently, she can be helped by repositioning so that her head tilts slightly backwards. Pressing the breast to allow the baby to breathe alters the shape of the nipple and should be avoided.

Breast-feeding should not hurt. The mother will feel comfortable when the baby is fixed correctly. This will tell her that her baby is feeding in the right position.

Taking the baby off the breast

The baby should be allowed to come off the breast by herself, when she has finished her feed. If she is not fixed correctly, however, the mother can put her finger into the corner of the baby's mouth to release the suction and then reposition her baby.

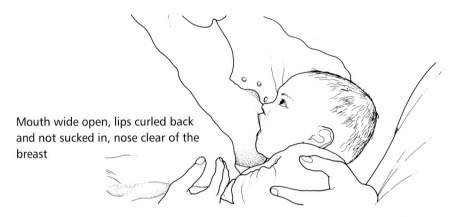

Mouth wide open, lips curled back and not sucked in, nose clear of the breast

The baby fixed correctly at the breast

Frequency and length of feeds
Breast milk production (or lactation) is more easily established if the baby feeds within the first four hours after delivery. Each baby is an individual and it is inappropriate to force her into a feeding routine for an adult's convenience. In the first few weeks of life, breast-feeding babies often feed as frequently as every one to two hours.

Some babies will get all the milk they require within five minutes, while others will take longer. It is important to let the baby decide the length of the feed so that she gets the rich, high-fat 'hind' milk that will satisfy her for longer. Feeding on demand limits the chances of the breasts becoming engorged or overfull with milk.

It is not necessary for the baby to feed from both breasts at each feed. However, offering the other breast at the next feed would seem sensible.

BENEFITS TO THE BABY FROM BREAST-FEEDING

■ Breast milk is suited to the baby's complete needs and digestion.
■ It is almost germ-free (straight from producer to consumer!).
■ The nutritional content of milk contains protective antibodies that are particularly effective against diarrhoea and vomiting. It is also thought to be helpful in the prevention of allergies.
■ A breast-fed baby gets more cuddles from her mother.
■ Breast milk has a varying composition, which keeps pace with the baby's growth and changing nutritional requirements.
■ It reduces the incidence and severity of food and respiratory allergies.

- Studies indicate a measurable increase in intelligence levels in babies who are breast-fed.

BENEFITS TO THE MOTHER

- Breast-feeding is thought to aid the mother–child relationship.
- It aids in the contraction of the womb.
- It reduces the risk of breast and ovarian cancers.
- It gives a sense of achievement of 'doing the best'.
- It is often less work when well established.
- It is cheap.

BREAST-FEEDING IN DAY CARE

Many mothers now wish to continue breast-feeding even though they plan to return to work. Being able to breast-feed means that a mother can remain close to her baby during her working day.

Early Years settings that care for very young babies should have a written policy on the promotion and management of breast-feeding, of which all staff are aware. Training in the skills necessary to support and encourage mothers, who wish to continue breast-feeding while their child is cared for away from home, is essential.

To allow a mother to continue to breast-feed means one of the following:

- The mother must work near to her baby's carer or nursery so she can come and feed when needed.
- Express breast milk should be given to the baby during her mother's absence.
- Partial breast-feeding – breast-feeding happens at the beginning and end of each day, with bottles of expressed breast or formula milk being given while the mother is at work.

Note: This last approach is only possible when lactation is well established. The breasts need regular stimulation to produce adequate supplies of milk, especially in the early days of feeding (see Table 4.1, pages 62–3).

Expressing breast milk

Necessary equipment/facilities needed will include the following:

- A pump – this works by producing a vacuum and a squeezing action over the areola, in a similar manner to the baby's jaws. Pumps can be hand, battery or mains electricity operated. The breasts must be stimulated in this way regularly during the day and night to maintain the milk supply. Milk can be expressed manually, but it will take much longer to produce the necessary amounts needed for several hours of separation between a mother and her baby.

- Sterile storage containers (bottles), teats and sterilising equipment.
- A vacuum cool bag to carry the expressed milk.
- A room with a door that can be locked, that is warm, private and clean, with a comfortable chair.
- Washing facilities for hands and equipment nearby.
- A storage facility for expressed milks, either a refrigerator or freezer, close by.

SAFE PRACTICE

- Expressed breast milk must be stored in sterile, covered containers, clearly labelled with the baby's name and dated.
- Expressed breast milk must be used within 24 hours if stored in a refrigerator and within 3 months from a freezer. It should be thoroughly defrosted before use and transported in a vacuum bag. Never keep it warm for bacteria to breed.
- Cleanliness and sterility of all equipment is as necessary for expressed breast milk as for formula milk – see Preparation of feeds and Procedure for giving a bottle, pages 65–8.

The role of the Early Years worker is to make a mother feel welcome, valued and supported in her decision to breast-feed. A mother will need privacy and time to feed her baby or to express her milk. Aim to make the experience both satisfying and successful for both mother and baby.

BREAST-FEEDING DIFFICULTIES

Table 4.1 lists the common difficulties in breast-feeding and how they can be overcome.

Table 4.1   Common breast-feeding difficulties

Problem	Cause	Management
Sore nipples	(a) Bad positioning (b) Nipples constantly wet (c) Infection such as thrush	(a) Check the baby's position at breast (b) Expose nipples to air Change breast pads frequently (c) Treatment for both baby and mother
Cracked nipples	Failure to manage sore nipples	Discontinue feeding Feed from other breast Treat superficial wounds sparingly with white soft paraffin or purified lanolin. Cover with breast pad

Engorgement (breasts over-full and painful)	(a) Excess blood supply in early days (b) Poor positioning (c) Inadequate removal of milk from breasts	(a) Baby-led feeding Bathing with hot and cold flannels (b) Check feeding technique (c) Use of firm bra Possibly manual removal of small amounts of milk
Blocked ducts (painful lumps in the breast, mother has no fever)	Poor feeding from baby or poor fixing	Correct fixing of the baby Regular, frequent feeds
Mastitis (infection or inflammation in a segment of the breast, possible fever)	Breast becoming overfull; inadequate feeding	Feed from affected side first Feed frequently Extra fluids to mother Bathe breasts with hot and cold flannels Possible treatment with antibiotics
Insufficient milk	(a) Poor fixing (b) Infrequent feeding (c) Use of complementary bottles (d) Poorly nourished and overtired mother	(a) Check positioning (b) Baby-led feeding (c) No bottles of milk (d) Support mother, give good diet amounts of rest and sufficient fluids
Unsettled baby	Wet, tired, abdominal pain; difficulty in fixing	Check physical comfort Additional support at feeding

Remember: What the mother eats will pass through her breast milk. This includes excess alcohol, all drugs and even nicotine.

Bottle-feeding

Cow's milk is ideal for calves, but it is not the natural food for babies. Bottled cow's milk, goat's milk and evaporated milk are unsuitable for babies under 6 months, and should preferably not be given before 12 months, because:

■ they contain high levels of curd protein (see below), which is difficult to digest
■ the high salt content is potentially dangerous for the immature kidneys of infants
■ the fat content contains a higher proportion of fatty acids, which are poorly absorbed and can hinder calcium absorption
■ the iron from cow's milk is poorly absorbed by humans.

Formula milks are recommended for babies in the first year of life who are not breast-fed. These are almost all cow's milk-based and have been changed by adapting the protein and fat contents, and by supplementing extra vitamins and minerals. The addition of iron is particularly important.

WHICH MILK TO CHOOSE

Formula milks are primarily **whey-dominant** or **curd-dominant**. Whey-dominant formulae contain the protein lactalbumin, which is easy for a baby to digest. These milks are particularly suited to the new baby and are nearest in composition to breast milk.

Hungrier babies may be given curd-dominant formula, which contains the protein casein. The curds in these milks take longer to digest and the baby feels fuller for longer.

However, there is no difference in the calorie or nutrient content of the two types of milk.

From 6 to 12 months, 'follow-on' milks have been developed to be used in place of cow's milk. These are less modified than new baby milks, but are again fortified with additional vitamins, iron and calcium.

Cow's milk intolerance

Some babies have difficulty in tolerating cow's milk products. This may be due to the specific protein or lactose (milk sugar) (see Chapter 6, pages 104–5). As a result milks have been developed in which the proteins from the soya bean have been used and the lactose has been changed to glucose. Medical advice should be sought prior to changing a baby to this type of formula to ensure that any symptoms are really due to an intolerance.

If **soya-based milk** is used, a baby may still develop a sensitivity to the protein. Care must also be taken with dental health as glucose is particularly harmful to healthy teeth – a cup should replace a bottle by 12 months to limit possible damage, if soya-based milk is used.

How to choose?

Advertising baby milks in the press or on television is forbidden by law. The biggest purchaser of baby milk is the National Health Service. As a result, mothers frequently continue with the milk their babies have been given in hospital.

Unless there is a strong reason to change, it is sensible for the baby to remain on this formula to allow her digestion and taste buds time to adjust. More information can be obtained from health visitors and baby clinics.

Activity

1 (a) Visit a chemist's shop, or a specialist mother and baby shop, and research the different types of feeding bottles and teats that are available.

   (b) Prepare a talk to your peers about the advantages and disadvantages of the different equipment you found.

(c) How can a new mother discover whether or not a manufacturer's claims for its formula milk are accurate?

2 Visit the local shops:

(a) What types of formula milk are available?

(b) Do they have age recommendations on them?

(c) Do they indicate if they are whey-based or curd-based?

(d) Do you think the instructions for making up the feeds are adequate?

(e) Are all the instructions in English, or can you find any with instructions in different languages?

(f) Look at the packaging. What might affect a carer's choice between the brands?

PREPARATION OF FEEDS

Keeping things clean

Cleanliness is very important in the preparation of baby feeds. Germs live and breed in a warm food such as milk, so personal hygiene is vital.

All equipment should be sterile and surfaces cleaned with very hot, soapy water. Sterilisation, usually using a chemical agent, means tanks and containers will need thorough washing every 24 hours and the correct concentration of solution made up (see the diagram on page 66). Chemical sterilisation is preferable to boiling. However, if boiling is the chosen method, everything must be boiled under the water for a full ten minutes. Steam sterilisers are effective and quick, but expensive.

What to do

The procedure for preparing a bottle-feed is shown in the diagram on page 68 (taken from Dare and O'Donovan, *Practical Guide to Working With Babies* (3rd edn), page 113).

Other non-chemical methods of sterilising equipment

■ Steam sterilisation – up to eight bottles take eight minutes and the method is very effective. Unit required costs approximately £30. Dangers of scalding from steam if unit is opened before cycle is complete.

■ Microwave sterilisation – up to four bottles in ten minutes using effective steam principle. Special unit essential, costing approximately £10 *plus* microwave oven. Not suitable for metal equipment.

■ Boiling – any numbers of bottles depending on the size of the saucepan. All equipment *must* be fully submerged with no air bubbles for a full ten minutes with the water at a rolling boil. Dangers of handling large quantities of boiling water must be considered carefully. This is a cheap method, with no expensive equipment required.

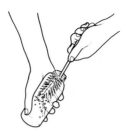

①Wash the bottles, teats and other equipment in hot water and detergent. Use a bottle brush for the inside of bottles. *Do not rub salt on the teats.* Squeeze boiled water through the teats.

②Rinse everything thoroughly in clean running water

③Fill the steriliser with clean, cold water. Add chemical solution. If in tablet form, allow to dissolve completely.

④Put the bottles, teats and other equipment (nothing metal) into the water. Ensure everything is covered by the water, with no bubbles. If necessary, weight down. Leave for the required time, according to manufacturer's instructions.

The procedure for sterilisation

SAFE PRACTICE

- Always follow the guidelines for sterilisation and cleanliness.
- Feeds should be prepared in a kitchen away from other small children.
- Boiling liquids must never be passed over a small baby.
- Always check the milk temperature before giving a baby a feed. A microwave oven is not suitable for the warming of bottles as they can produce unexpected 'hot spots'.

How much feed does a baby need?

The calculation for the nutritional needs of small babies is: 75 ml of fully reconstituted feed for every 500 g of the baby's weight in 24 hours (2½ fl oz per lb of body weight x 24 hours). The total feed is then divided into the number of bottles it is likely the baby will take in that time. For a newborn, it is usually eight feeds.

- Every baby is an individual and, like breast-feeding, a schedule should be 'baby-led' to allow for changes in appetite.
- Inaccuracy in making up feeds is a widespread problem, so take care.
- Over-concentration leads to excessive weight gain, too much salt and possible strain on the baby's kidneys.
- Cereals and sugars should never be added to bottles.
- Under-concentration is less common, but it can lead to poor weight gain, constipation and a distressed, hungry baby.

PROCEDURE FOR GIVING A BOTTLE

- Wash your hands.
- Collect all equipment for the feed, before picking up the baby. Place the bottle on a tray and cover the bottle. Keep it warm in a jug of hot water. Put the bib, tissues and any other articles you need ready too.
- Change the baby and make her comfortable. Wash your hands.
- Take the baby to the feeding area and sit in a comfortable position. This is a time for talking to and cuddling with the baby, and should be enjoyable, for both of you, not to be rushed. Maintain eye contact and hold the baby firmly to give her a sense of security.
- Test the temperature of the milk against the inside of your wrist.
- Test the size of the teat by turning the bottle upside down. The milk should flow freely at first – several drops per second.
- Stimulate the rooting reflex, by gently touching the baby's lips with the teat, and then place the teat over her tongue and into her mouth.
- Check that milk is always present in the teat. This stops the baby sucking on air and becoming frustrated at not receiving feed. Gentle tension on the teat helps the baby to keep sucking steadily.
- A feed usually takes about 20 minutes with a break after about 10 minutes to bring up the baby's wind (see below). After a feed, let the wind come up again.
- Change the baby again, if necessary, and settle her comfortably and safely.
- Clear away, wash utensils thoroughly and re-sterilise.

REMEMBER!

- A baby should *never* be propped up with a bottle. Choking can easily occur.
- Siblings and unsure adults will need supervision at all times when feeding.
- Bottles are for milk or cooled, boiled water – never add solids.

Preparing the bottle-feed

① Check that the formula has not passed its sell-by date. Read the instructions on the tin. Ensure the tin has been kept in a cool, dry cupboard.

② Boil some *fresh* water and allow to cool.

③ Wash hands and nails thoroughly.

④ Gather together the sterilised equipment. Rinse with cool, boiled water if a sterilising tank has been used.

⑤ Fill bottle, or a jug if making a large quantity, to the required level with water.

⑥ Measure the exact amount of powder using the scoop provided. Level with a sterile knife. Do not pack down.

⑦ Add the powder to the measured water in the bottle or jug.

⑧ Screw cap on bottle and shake, or mix well in the jug and pour into sterilised bottles.

⑨ If not using immediately, cool quickly and store in the fridge. If using immediately, hold the bottle under cold running water, then test the temperature on the inside of your wrist and use straight away.

⑩ Babies will take cold milk but they prefer warm food (as from the breast). If you wish to warm ready prepared milk, place bottle in a jug of hot water, test the temperature and use immediately. Whenever a bottle is left for short periods, or stored in the fridge, cover with the cap provided.

⑪ It is best practice to make up fresh formula for each feed, and to throw away any leftover milk after each feed. Storing made-up formula milk may increase the chance of a baby becoming ill and should be avoided.

The Department of Health advice on feeding away from home:

It's safest to carry a sealed flask of just boiled water and add fresh formula milk powder when needed. The water must still be hot (70 degrees centigrade) when you use it. Alternatively, ready-to-drink infant formula milk may be used when away from home. If it's not possible to follow the advice, or if you need to transport a feed – for example to a nursery or childminder – you should prepare the feed at home and cool it in the back of the fridge. Remove just before you leave and carry in a cool bag with an ice pack. Use within four hours, or if you reach your destination within four hours, take it out of the cool bag and store it at the back of the fridge. Feeds should never be stored for longer than 24 hours although this length of time is no longer considered ideal, especially for young babies. It's always safer to make up a fresh feed whenever possible.

WINDING A BABY

Many old wives' tales are linked with bringing up a baby's wind.
- Air rises naturally in an upright bottle, so the baby should also be held upright. This helps nature.
- Apply gentle, but firm pressure to the baby's stomach. This can be by the heel of your hand if the baby is on the your lap, or by the front of your body if you are standing.
- Gently rub the baby's back.

This procedure should result in natural winding.

If winding does not take place within a few seconds, it will mean that the air has continued down the gastric tract and will be expelled in the nappy. Babies often release wind without any help and only become distressed with an adult's efforts to help.

IS THE BABY HAVING ENOUGH FOOD?

This is a question often asked by anxious carers, whether the baby is breast-fed or bottle-fed. Consider the following when deciding:
- appearance and general behaviour
- weight gain – this should be 130–170 g (6–8 oz) per week for the first four months (breast-fed babies lose more weight after birth than bottle-fed babies, but this is made up by 10 to 14 days)
- alertness when awake, and falling asleep following a period of calm, after a feed
- warmth and silkiness of the skin; it should be firm and elastic to touch
- pinkness of mucous membranes

- whether the abdomen is prominent (but not distended) after feeds
- whether the baby moves and kicks well, cries for food (or if cold or insecure), but does not have prolonged crying spells
- whether the baby sleeps well between feeds
- whether urine and stools are passed easily without discomfort.

REMEMBER!

- Bottle-fed babies' stools are putty coloured, formed and faecal smelling.
- Breast-fed babies' stools are inoffensive, mustard-coloured and very soft.

Weighing

Although this is an important sign of growth and sufficient food, remember that babies will have spurts in gaining weight.

Variation in the times of day the baby is weighed, the accuracy of the scales, variations between scales, whether the baby is clothed or naked, whether the baby is weighed before or after a feed, will all play a part in differences and unexpected changes in weight.

BOTTLE-FEEDING IN DAY CARE

Many parents and carers are asked to bring their own reconstituted formula milk for their baby to the nursery or childminder. If this is the practice in your nursery, check the following:

- The bottles should be labelled clearly with the child's name to avoid any possible confusion, and dated; they are transported safely by an insulated carrier bag; they are stored at the correct temperature in a clean, regularly defrosted refrigerator.
- Charts should be kept of how much milk a baby takes at each feed and the baby's key worker gives the information to the parent at the end of the day.
- Babies should always be fed according to any medical advice, and the wishes and cultural preferences of the parents are fully respected.
- Procedures for emergency milk supplies should be arranged and known by all staff.

Weaning

When a baby is no longer satisfied with breast or formula milk and is taking large quantities of fluids, then weaning (the introduction of solid foods) may be considered.

The following advice is given to parents by the Food Standards Agency:

In recent years the advice about when to start babies on solid foods has changed. This is because we now know more about when babies are ready for starting solid foods and the effects of giving solid foods too early. We now know that it's usually best to wait until 6 months, but all babies are different so you might want to ask your health visitor or GP for advice about when is best for your baby.

Why wait until six months?
Giving solid foods to a baby before he or she can cope with them can increase the risk of infection and allergies.

By 6 months, babies are physically ready to start eating solid foods. At this age, babies can sit up with support, control their heads and move food around their mouths. Their digestive and immune systems are also stronger and they are often interested in food and want to chew. At this age babies need more than milk alone.

If your baby still seems to be hungry on their usual milk feeds before 6 months, try offering more milk at each bottle feed if they are finishing the bottle and seem to be looking for more. If you are breastfeeding, try feeding more often.

If you're concerned about your baby's health, or you want to start your baby on solid foods before 6 months, talk to your health visitor or GP first.

AIMS OF WEANING

■ To make the baby less nutritionally dependent on milk. For the baby at the age of 1 year, milk should provide about 40 per cent of the calorie intake. So, it still remains an important food source for the toddler.
■ To provide a variety of textures, purées and dices, which will enable the baby to join in family meals, so aiding her social and intellectual development.
■ To establish the acceptance of a variety of foods and flavours, setting healthy eating patterns throughout childhood.
■ To introduce iron into the diet. Human and unfortified cow's milks are poor sources of this mineral. During the first few months an infant has sufficient iron reserves received from her mother. However, after around 6 months of age, these reserves become run down and foods with good iron contents are needed in the diet.
■ To introduce a cup and spoon to the baby.
■ To provide and extend the learning experience for the baby by introducing wider tastes, textures, smells, temperatures, consistencies and to promote fine physical skills and help social development.

Babies should be introduced to textured foods gradually. The first foods should be smooth and runny. The Food Standards Agency recommends mixing a teaspoon of one of the following with the baby's usual milk:

■ smooth vegetable purée such as carrot, parsnip, potato or yam, or
■ fruit purée such as banana, cooked apple, pear or mango, or
■ cereal (not wheat-based) such as baby rice, sago, maize, cornmeal or millet.

Over the following weeks and months, babies will move from puréed food to mashed food, and eventually on to chopped food.

MANAGING THE WEANING PROCESS

Many mothers worry about this aspect of child rearing, so it is especially important that the carer is calm and confident herself. Weaning is an ongoing process that the baby, parents and carers learn together.

It helps to remember that the nutritional content of early weaning is less important than the baby beginning to discover and accept different flavours and textures.

In any learning process a baby should not be too tired or too hungry. She will not yet realise that the contents of the spoon will satisfy her as the bottle or breast does, so some milk may be given before the spoon to help settle her. Allow plenty of time for her new experience and promote a relaxed atmosphere. The morning or early afternoon feeds are good times for introducing something new.

First weaning foods should be:

■ gluten-free
■ sugar-free
■ salt-free

Use a sterilised, plastic spoon with a flat bowl that allows the baby to suck the contents off easily and initially offer a half to one teaspoon of a bland, warm savoury food.

After this first introduction the same food can be offered the next day – too many new tastes at one time can confuse a small baby and if something upsets her it is easier to discover the cause. Refusal may not mean dislike of the food itself, but of the new experience or the texture.

After two or three days, when the baby is used to the new flavour and consistency, another food can be tried. If the first chosen weaning food is a baby cereal, the next food could be a purée of fruit or vegetable, for example a purée of carrots. Babies appear to enjoy the very bland nature of cereals and there is a risk of a baby becoming overweight if too much is given.

As the quantity of solid food a baby eats increases, the amounts of milk offered may be gradually reduced so that by about the fifth week of weaning one of the milk feeds can be completely replaced by solids. As the milk is reduced, the baby will be thirsty and cool boiled water in a bottle (never sweet drinks that can cause dental decay) should be given. Diluted pure fruit juices can be offered by a spoon and cup, egg cup or training beaker.

KEY POINTS

- Supervision is important in weaning to limit the dangers of choking.
- Worries over salmonella mean it is no longer recommended that eggs, the white or the yolk, are used as weaning foods, and eggs should not now be part of a baby's diet until after one year of age.

As the baby becomes more actively involved, let her 'help' by holding a spoon as well. A baby can discover the textures and temperatures of her food with her fingers, as well as developing co-ordination skill in getting food into her mouth. Babies enjoy this part of meal times. Inevitably, a mess can occur, so plan for this with bibs and protection of carpets, etc. and allow her plenty of time. Learning to cope with lumps, experiencing different tastes and textures, developing hand-eye skills and eating in family groups are just as important as the nutritional aspect of weaning and should be encouraged. Always talk to her at meal times and try to widen her vocabulary by introducing new words such as 'hot', 'cold', 'thick', etc.

Activity
Make a list of new words that might be said to a baby of 9 months during lunch time. What early maths and science ideas might be introduced at this time?

KEY POINT

Research tells us that babies who are discouraged from playing with their foods, from developing the skills of self-feeding and those who are not offered different textured foods, may have related eating and other difficulties later in childhood. These may include difficulty in tolerating lumps, food refusal and dislike of messy play activities.

Each baby is an individual and some take to weaning more easily than others. One baby of 6 months may effortlessly accept a spoon and new foods, while another many not be ready. Ensure that you offer the baby the opportunity and make it a relaxed and pleasurable experience. Let the baby set the pace.

Vitamin supplements
Current advice is to give children vitamin drops with vitamins A, C and D from the age of 1 to 5 years old. Breast-fed babies, and babies drinking less than 500ml of infant formula milk per day, should begin vitamin drops at 6 months. Health visitors will advise parents about this.

Cleanliness of weaning equipment

Sterilisation is no longer essential, as social cleanliness – a high standard of personal and domestic hygiene – is sufficient from 9 months. However, the baby should have her own bowl, mug etc., which is kept for her sole use. Everything can now be washed thoroughly in a sink or a dishwasher. The exception remains for bottles that have contained milk. These should continue to be sterilised, as stale milk is a good source for bacterial growth and so a potential threat to health.

Babies with special needs

Babies with special needs may have difficulty in coping with either the amount or the consistency of a food and with swallowing.

Activity
Make a list of new words that might be introduced to a baby of 12 months during lunch time. What maths and science ideas might be learnt during this time?

RESTRICTIONS ON WEANING DIETS

When weaning their baby some parents wish to follow their own dietary codes, which can be affected by religious, cultural or personal beliefs.

Vegetarian diets

A baby whose parents do not wish her to eat meat or fish will need to be weaned using a combination of cereals, beans and seeds, dairy and soya produce, fruit and vegetables.

Nuts, which are a good source of protein, should only be offered as ground nuts from 1 year and preferably not until 3 years.

Quorn and textured vegetable protein (TVP) are unsuitable for babies as their salt content is too high.

Vegan diets

Diets for babies where no animal or fish flesh, or animal products, are allowed are challenging and you will need expert dietary advice. This will help to ensure that a nutritionally balanced diet can be achieved that includes sufficient calcium, vitamin B_{12} and protein for the developing baby.

Hindus and Sikhs

Fish, meat and eggs, and foods containing them, are not permitted.

Muslims

Meat used must be killed by the halal method and there are some weaning foods on the market that now meet this criterion. Pork and pork products are not permitted.

Jews

Pork and pork products are not permitted and other meat must be kosher, from specialist butchers. Fish, which have fins and scales, can be used but not shellfish and eels. Any other products must be checked to ensure that animal products that are not kosher have not been used in processing, for example, biscuits made with animal fat and cheese containing rennet.

Chinese

Usually dairy products are excluded.

In the NHS publication 'Weaning: Starting solid foods' the following advice is given about which foods to avoid as they may be harmful to babies:

SALT (which contains sodium)
Do not add any salt to foods for babies. Do not use stock cubes or gravy in your baby's food as they are often high in salt. When you are
cooking for the family, do not add salt, so your baby can share the family foods.

SUGAR
Sugar can encourage a sweet tooth and lead to tooth decay when first teeth start to come through. Try mashed banana, breast or formula milk to sweeten food if necessary.

HONEY
Don't give honey until your baby is 1 year old. Very occasionally, it can contain a type of bacteria, which can produce toxins in the baby's intestines and can cause a very serious illness (infant botulism). Remember that honey is also a sugar and can lead to tooth decay.

NUTS
Whole nuts, including peanuts, should not be given to children under 5 years in case of choking.

LOW-FAT FOODS
Low-fat foods, whether yoghurt, fromage frais, cheese or fat spreads, are not suitable for babies or children under 2. Fat is an important source of calories and some vitamins which they need.

REMEMBER TO CHECK THE FOOD LABEL.

WEANING PLANS

A suggested weaning plan is shown in Table 4.2 opposite.

- Wash the baby's hands before and after meals.
- Is the baby comfortable?
- Is the baby well supervised?
- Do not add salt or sugar.
- Test food temperature with a separate sterilised spoon – no blowing or putting your finger in your food.
- Check for bones in fish and pips in fruit.
- Remove bib after meals.
- Modified milks should be used until the baby is 1 year old.

Activity

As a professional childcare worker you will be expected to have wide knowlege to meet the needs of a variety of different families.

1 Make three weaning plans (see Table 4.2) for babies in your care. These plans should be for the first year of life and should demonstrate the changes the baby will encounter during the first year in sucking, chewing and coping with lumps, etc.
   (a) Make one plan for a baby whose parents wish her to be a vegetarian.
   (b) Make one plan for a baby whose parents are Asian Muslims.
   (c) Make one plan for a baby whose parents are of African-Carribean origin.

You will need to research widely the dietary and nutritional requirements of each of these plans. Visit libraries, child health cinics, the health visiting service and community dietician for information.

2 How do you think the foods in the plans you made above might differ from the weaning plan in Table 4.2 opposite?
3 How easily could you meet the cultural and religious wishes of these families?
4 Did you find that baby food manufacturers are responsive to the needs of the variety of customs and cultures in our society?
5 Check and comment on the nutritional content of commercial baby foods from their labels. Take notice of any 'hidden' sugars or salt.
6 Write a report justifying your selections, based on cost, nutritional needs and parental choices. Did you find it difficult to meet these needs?
7 Visit your nearest health centre and determine your Local Authority infant feeding policy. How does it reflect the specific nutritional customs and practices of the local community?

Table 4.2 The weaning stages – a suggested weaning plan

Stages	1	2	3	4	5	6
On waking	Breast or bottle-feed	Breast or bottle-feed	Breast or bottle-feed	Breast or bottle-feed	Breast or bottle-feed	Breast or bottle-feed/cup
Breakfast	1–2 teaspoons baby rice mixed with milk from feed or with water; breast or bottle-feed	2 teaspoon baby rice mixed with milk from feed or with water; breast or bottle-feed	Baby rice or cereal mixed with milk from feed or with water or puréed banana; breast or bottle-feed	Cereal mixed with milk from feed or with water; fruit, toast fingers spread with unsalted butter	Cereal, fish or fruit; toast fingers; milk	Cereal and milk; fish, yoghurt or fruit; toast and milk
Lunch	Breast or bottle-feed	1–2 teaspoon purée or sieved vegetables, or vegetables and chicken; breast or bottle-feed	Puréed or sieved meat or fish and vegetables, or proprietary food; followed by 2 teaspoons puréed fruit or prepared baby dessert; drink of cooled, boiled water or well-diluted juice (from a cup)	Finely minced meat or mashed fish, with mashed vegetables; mashed banana or stewed fruit or milk pudding; drink of cooled boiled water or well-diluted juice in a cup	Mashed fish, minced meat or cheese with vegetables; milk pudding or stewed fruit; drink	Well-chopped meat, liver or fish or cheese with mashed vegetables; milk pudding or fruit fingers; drink
Tea	Breast or bottle-feed	Breast or bottle-feed	Puréed fruit or baby dessert; breast or bottle-feed	Toast with cheese or savoury spread; breast or bottle-feed	Bread and butter sandwiches with savoury spread or seedless jam; sponge finger or biscuit; milk drink	Fish, cheese or pasta; sandwiches; fruit; milk drink
Late evening	Breast or bottle-feed	Breast or bottle-feed	Breast or bottle-feed, if necessary			

Remember! The Food Standards Agency now advises parents not to wean babies before the age of 6 months unless recommended by a health visitor or doctor. For regularly updated information, visit www.eatwell.org.uk/agesandstages/baby/weaning.

REMEMBER!

Age 4–6 months, offer sieved or puréed food.
Age 6–8 months, offer mashed and finger foods.
Age 8–9 months, offer chopped foods.
A baby who is breast-fed has her nutritional needs fully met until she is at least 6 months – weaning is not recommended before this.

Possible feeding difficulties

Table 4.3 lists the main problems associated with feeding and how they may be managed.

Table 4.3   Problems associated with feeding

Problem	Signs and symptoms	Management
Allergies and intolerances	Faltering growth, diarrhoea and vomiting, infantile eczema/general rashes, wheezing	Liaise with medical advice/dietician Breast-feed if possible Use cow's milk replacement, for example, soya milk
Constipation	Small, hard, infrequent stools	Increase fluid intake Ensure feed not too concentrated No laxatives or sugar in feeds If weaned, increase fruit or vegetable intake Check to exclude underfeeding
Diarrhoea	Frequent, loose, watery stools	Check hygiene of food preparation Give clear fluids and seek medical advice
Colic	Babies of (usually) less than 3 months cry and draw legs up, appearing to have abdominal pain. Often show distress at the same time of day – frequently early evening	Cause unknown Feed baby Check teat for size and flow, if bottle-fed Monitor feeding technique Reassure carer that pain is self-limiting Comfort baby with movement and cuddling Seek advice from health visitor
Overfeeding	Baby vomits/unsettled, passes large stools, sore buttocks, excessive weight gain	Seek clinic/health visitor advice Check re-constitution of feeds

Table 4.3 (*continued*)

Possetting	Baby frequently vomits small amounts, but gains weight and is happy	Condition self-limiting; usually solved when baby is upright and walking Monitor weight
Underfeeding	Baby very hungry, wakes and cries; stools small and dark, poor weight gain; vomiting as a result of crying and air swallowing	Ensure feeds are correctly re-constituted If breast-feeding, check technique and mother's diet Increase frequency of feeds, before quantities

REMEMBER!

Diarrhoea and vomiting can be serious in small babies, whatever the reason, and medical advice should be sought.

QUICK CHECK

1 Describe the nutritional advantages to an infant of breast-feeding.
2 How can the successful production of breast milk be undermined?
3 A mother complains her nipples are sore when breast-feeding. What advice might you offer?
4 Which mineral is stored in the baby's liver for use during the first few months of life?
5 A mother asks how much weight her new baby should be gaining. How would you reply?
6 How would you reassure a mother who is worried that her breast milk, after four weeks' breast-feeding, looks watery?
7 A mother bottle-feeding a 4-week-old baby asks how much feed should be offered. What would you answer?
8 Describe the main hygiene principles that must be used for safe bottle-feeding.
9 What specific safety factors should be remembered when weaning a baby?
10 What might lead you to suspect that a baby was being underfed?
11 How could you help a baby who was having colic?
12 'Weaning is a learning process.' Explain what you understand by this.
13 What special precautions are needed when giving eggs to a baby as part of a weaning diet?
14 Why is a microwave oven unsuitable for warming babies' bottles?
15 Describe how a baby who is being bottle-fed should be held.

5 NUTRITION AND THE GROWING CHILD

This chapter covers:
- ■ **Mealtimes for children**
- ■ **Nutrition for toddlers**
- ■ **Nutrition for children with special needs**
- ■ **Preventing food fads and minor eating problems**

Mealtimes for children

The issue of food carries with it both power and emotion. A mother who lovingly shops for organic foods, prepares, cooks and presents a healthy meal to a toddler may understandably find it difficult to be relaxed if he spits it out. The mother may feel as rejected as the food.

When organising mealtimes for young children, the person who provides the food is also likely to be the controller of what is offered. So, if a carer dislikes vegetables and fresh fruits, for example, that carer may either not provide them or give out hidden messages to a young child that they

Phrases from childhood

are 'not good'. Never expect a small child to eat what you will not eat yourself. Also, if a carer's own knowledge of basic nutrition is limited, that carer may inadvertently offer a poorly balanced diet.

We therefore bring our own eating patterns to feeding children. Do any of the quotations on page 81 remind you of your childhood?

So, food is much more complex than just providing fuel for the body. It can become a sign to the outside world of a 'good' carer. To some people, this will be a bouncing, large child, while to others it would mean a slim, possibly underweight, child. Carers often boast that their children 'will eat everything'. Others may be reluctant to let their children go to parties where there might be 'junk food' and so limit a child's opportunity for social development.

Whatever our backgrounds and previous experiences, it is difficult to be calm about food and children.

CHANGING PATTERNS

Our eating habits have changed over the years. Why?
■ We have more labour-saving machinery.
■ We are less active, using cars and buses more, and exercising less, and as a result can more easily become overweight.
■ Modern technology and ease of importing produce means we can have almost any food all year round, for example, strawberries, mangoes, kiwi fruit.
■ We are busy and have less time to shop, cook and eat our foods, especially in a relaxed family setting.
■ As a nation we eat too many fatty and sugary foods from convenience sources.
This all affects how we plan and organise food for children.

Mealtime can be a wonderful opportunity for a family or nursery to have a pleasurable time together – perhaps to discuss the day's events, learn new words, have new experiences and develop healthy attitudes to food.

Most children respond to a regular routine of mealtimes and constant snacking ('grazing') can be detrimental to a healthy appetite, limiting the opportunity for eating important body-building foods.

REMEMBER!

■ A snack to an adult may be the equivalent of a meal to a child.
■ Check that food is not used instead of attention, for example giving a child a packet of crisps to eat while watching television.
■ Avoid using food as a bribe or a reward.

■ The adult is a role model in diet.
■ Young children need three meals a day and usually two or three small
  healthy snacks (see Healthy snacks, Chapter 3, page 45).

WHEN TO EAT

Timing of meals is important. A child may be too tired to take advantage of a heavy meal at the end of the day. A main meal at midday is preferable, plus the usual recommended snacks – children need regular 'fuel' during the day to cope with their activity.

Meals should not be hurried. A child at nursery is learning new skills of handling cutlery, tasting new foods and textures, extending language and being introduced to the social custom of group eating. The child may start by eating his favourite or known food and be rushed into leaving what may be more important nutritionally. He may use different utensils at home or come from a culture where eating with fingers is the norm. All children may be faced with unfamiliar foods and smells, and time is needed to help them to respond to new situations.

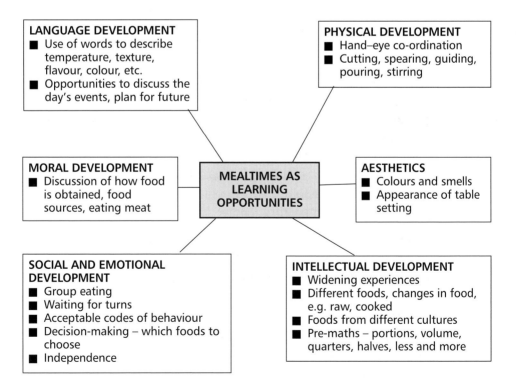

Mealtimes as learning opportunities

- Mealtimes should be relaxed and unhurried.
- Avoid distractions, no television or games during meals – this should be a time for talking and listening.
- Set food out attractively and make sure the child is comfortable.
- A child eats best in company, so try and always sit down and eat with him.
- Encourage him to wash his hands before meals.
- Offer a variety of foods, and foods from different cultures.
- Try not to overfill his plate, but offer seconds.
- Remember a child's appetite will vary from day to day.
- Consider the timing of the main meal; tiredness and illness can reduce appetite, and exercise stimulate it.
- Offer water to drink with meals.
- Encourage careful eating and cutlery or tool use, but do not place undue emphasis on manners, as it is best for the child to learn from your example.
- Foods that are refused are often accepted at another time.
- Nutritional needs can be met in a variety of ways.
- Offer a child some choice within the food groups.
- Occasional sweets and junk foods do no harm.
- Food should never be used as a bribe or punishment.

REMEMBER!

It is easier to form healthy attitudes to food than to change poor habits.

Activity

Plan for lunch time with children at nursery:
1. Ask the children to design a table cloth, either by decorating a paper one or by painting or printing a plain cotton sheet. Suggest they choose a colour or topic theme.
2. Decorate napkins and paper beakers to match.
3. Illustrate menus, for example with pictures of different foods.
4. Arrange posies of flowers for centre pieces.
5. Show the children how to set the table with accuracy.

Nutrition for toddlers

The nutritional principles for toddlers are as for all young children. They have high levels of energy and are growing fast so they need the correct balance of nutrients (see Chapter 2). Calorie-dense foods from fats play an important part in their diet, but after the age of 2 years it is recommended that the daily fat intake be reduced to 30 per cent of the total calorie intake.

REMEMBER!

- Three small, regular, high-quality meals plus two snacks – between 1200 and 1400 kcal daily.
- One pint of whole milk daily.
- Vitamin supplements A, D and C.
- Monitor iron intakes.
- Gradual introduction to wider foods and textures, including spices and pulses.
- No added salt or sugar.
- Give only ground nuts until the age of 5. Check for peanut allergy.
- The amount of food eaten may vary from day to day – large volumes one day to almost negligible at others, this is normal.
- Likes and dislikes also vary from day to day.
- Too much reliance on one food can lead to nutritional imbalance, for example too high an intake of milk.

Between the ages of 1 and 2 a child is rapidly developing new skills and is keen to use them. Although he will be able to use a spoon, he may drop food or turn the spoon over before it reaches his mouth.

A child will use his fingers to supplement spoons. He may spill his drink. The language he has to illustrate and explain his needs is limited – 50 to 100 words by 2 years. However his understanding is much wider. He

The toddler is rapidly developing new skills and is keen to practise them

is aware of his developing power over his world and is keen to gain independence. All this means that mealtimes can be demanding for carers and possibly frustrating for the toddler.

Plan for mess and ensure the toddler is secure in a harness in his high chair. Try to provide equipment to aid his independence, such as flat-bowled spoons, plastic bowls fixed by suction to the high chair trays and beakers with two handles. He may still need a bottle for comfort at bed time, but only for water or milk. However, by the age of 2 many children no longer use bottles. Feeding beakers are unneccessary as they require a sucking action rather than teaching a drinking action. Drinks given in an egg cup during bath time can help the child to practise adult drinking and make spills easier to manage – don't let him drink the bath water though!

Allow the toddler to practise his emerging skills – it will take time and tolerance. Even if he appears inefficient at feeding himself, he is gaining valuable skills and experience. Taking over may provoke frustration and a negative response from the toddler, who is finding that he has choice and power, and a 'No' from a toddler at mealtimes will not be changed by food being forced on him. It is both professionally unacceptable and probably unsuccessful – even if food reaches his mouth, he will be unlikely to swallow it and this may even lead to a more serious long-term eating problem.

As with older children, a toddler enjoys eating in company and occasionally from his carer's plate. A child learns partly by imitation and will be less likely to encroach on an adult's plate if he is allowed to have time experimenting with the process of eating from his own plate or bowl. This may mean feeling the texture and temperature of foods with his fingers, testing the consistency and occasionally seeing if food fits in his ears and nose too!

Allow the toddler to feel the texture and temperature of foods with his fingers

As long as the carer expects some mess and tries to be relaxed, never forcing food or displaying disgust, this can be thought of as a normal development.

A toddler may have periods of food refusal, spitting out what were previously accepted foods and showing a reluctance to sit at the table. Here the toddler is demonstrating his developing power over his own environment and understanding how to use it. A positive response is to accept it as a 'phase' and ensure that he is not filling up on inappropriate snacks, that meal timings are suitable and accept that he will eat when he is hungry. Unacceptable foods should not be hidden in other, preferred foods as this undermines trust and may result in familiar and nutritious foods being discarded.

Avoid battles over food – they prolong the situation and mealtimes can then become distressing for everyone. A carer can never make a child eat and, if food is forced upon him, the child may not swallow it or may even vomit. A child can miss the odd meal and still remain healthy, and he will always eat when he is hungry.

SAFE PRACTICE

- Chewing may be hurried or immature, so always check for hard lumps, bones and any whole nuts – *supervise*.
- Never leave a toddler unattended – use a fixed harness in a high chair.
- Do not use drinking glasses as pieces can be bitten out.
- Always check the temperature of food.

Nutrition for children with special needs

Some children, particularly those with cerebral palsy, may have problems in eating. These difficulties can become more pronounced when solid foods are introduced. Such a child may have difficulties with swallowing, and in releasing his bite and grasp reflexes. In addition, he may experience spasms of the neck muscles, with arching of the back, which makes positioning difficult.

An inability to cope with either the amount or the consistency of a food may lead to choking. So when new types of food are introduced, it should be done slowly and gradually, with supervision and a knowledge of first aid. Finger foods and foods of a sloppy consistency are best to start with, gradually moving to foods of a firmer texture. Try not to have foods that break up easily, such as crumbly biscuits.

Adjust the child's sitting position before a meal so his head is in midline, with his arms stretched across the table and his feet flat on the floor or on the high chair foot support. Place the cutlery on the table or tray so he can try to pick them up. Sit at his side and help him only if needed, encouraging his independence and praising his effort.

GOOD PRACTICE

Even though mealtimes may take longer, it is important for the child's self-esteem to learn to feed himself, if possible. All children benefit from the handling of food – learning texture, consistency, shape and temperature. Children with special needs also gain from this sensory experience.

REMEMBER!

Children with special needs also have likes and dislikes, and variations in appetite.

USEFUL EQUIPMENT

- ■ Tough plastic spoons with large, rounded handles.
- ■ Heavy, flat, round feeding dishes with wide bases.
- ■ Non-slip mats to prevent equipment sliding.
- ■ Two-handled mugs.
- ■ Weighted trainer mugs (readily available from chemists).
- ■ Straws – these are sometimes are easier to manage than a mug or a cup.

As with any child, encouragement, a pleasant atmosphere and company help to make mealtimes enjoyable. If the child has to be fed, again ensure he is sitting correctly and comfortably. Feed him slowly and carefully, especially if he has poor control of his throat muscles and there is a risk of choking. Cut the food into small pieces and place it on the back of his tongue to ease swallowing. Check for hard lumps, fish bones, etc. Always tell the child what you are giving him, and try to offer choices.

Mouth hygiene is important and should be included in the daily routine. Teeth cleaning provides an opportunity for enhancing an awareness of the lips, tongue and teeth. Rinsing and spitting out is a good exercise for weak lip and tongue muscles.

Preventing food fads and minor eating problems

Nutrition for young children is an emotive issue for many carers. It provokes feelings of inadequacy and rejection when difficulties occur. Setting and developing good habits are much easier than attempting to change entrenched eating patterns – see Good Practice, page 84.

A child who has previously eaten well can show sudden upset when there are changes in her life. New schools, new babies, illnesses and temporary separation from prime carers can all upset a child's eating pattern, which usually settles of its own accord if not over-stressed. Knowing about such changes can help you to manage any feeding problems. Try not to introduce unfamiliar foods at these times.

An over-emphasis on table manners and a reluctance to allow toddlers to make a mess when eating can lead to food refusal. Sometimes a carer may be unaware that small children can be messy when eating and feel that a child in their care is abnormal. If a child eats on her own, she may wish to finish as quickly as possible in order to rejoin her friends and so may develop a poor appetite.

Set a maximum time limit to meals, never longer than 30 minutes – then remove any uneaten foods calmly. Allowing the tension to rise as a child sits miserably over a meal is unlikely to be successful and everyone becomes upset. Never prepare special foods as an alternative to a meal that you know is usually acceptable to a child, but has been refused, and do not use pudding as a bribe to force a child to eat their main course.

It is important to praise and encourage a child trying new and different foods. If she is experiencing minor eating difficulties, a negative attitude to these new foods may otherwise develop. Older children can be encouraged by involving them in shopping, cooking and setting tables, as well as some choice in menu selection.

Carers keen on 'healthy' diets need to ensure that no undue emphasis is placed on specific foods, for example by identifying foods as 'good' or 'bad', such as white versus brown bread. Toddlers in particular will sense any emotional tension from carers during mealtimes. A matter-of-fact approach to food fads and refusal is usually most effective. Additional attention for a child who is refusing food only creates or prolongs a potential problem, however, a child eating widely and well should always be praised.

Ensure that food is not used to replace attention – a story at the end of the day rather than a chocolate bar will be more beneficial to a child's development.

Try and always maintain a calm manner and approach at mealtimes, and, again, think carefully if you are unreasonably trying to impose your own dietary views, likes and dislikes on a child, if so any apparent problems may be yours and not the child's. It is interesting that children identified as having eating problems often manage quite happily in groups situation away from the emotional tension and anxiety of their carers. Acknowledging and supporting carers through difficult times over food refusal may be beneficial in reducing stress levels for the child too.

REMEMBER!

- Children's appetites vary.
- Children have food likes and dislikes, which should be respected.
- It is important to distinguish between the child who needs less food than the average and the child who refuses food as a part of her growing independence.
- A balanced diet can usually be achieved by meeting nutritional needs from other food sources, for example yoghurt instead of cheese for calcium.

DO YOU NEED HELP?

The following are signs that you should seek professional help with an eating problem:

- when a child is not gaining weight
- when a child does not reach milestones of development, and is not happy and sociable
- when a child is not fit, lacks energy and suffers from recurrent illness (see Faltering growth, Chapter 8, pages 130–4).

Where to seek help
The health visitor and GP would usually be able to advise on minor food problems and meal management. If the difficulties become serious you will be referred to a Child Guidance Clinic and psychological help may be sought.

Activity
Select a group of 5 year olds and ask them to describe their favourite foods. What do they say? Is it as you expected?
Note: Children often have healthy food favourites that might surprise you.

QUICK CHECK

1 What do you understand by the phrase 'food as a power tool'?
2 List 5 ways in which our eating patterns have changed over the last 20 years.

3   Explain the term 'grazing'.
4   Explain what you understand by the phrase 'Meal times are a learning experience'.
5   What can affect a child's appetite?
6   What are the special nutritional requirements for a toddler?
7   Why would a knowledge of first aid be important at mealtimes for children with special needs?
8   How do toddlers learn to develop acceptable meal-time behaviour?
9   How would you manage a toddler's food fads?
10   List the signs that would indicate that a child's growth is faltering.
11   How can carers pass on negative attitudes to food?
12   What choice of cutlery would help a child with special needs to develop independence in feeding?
13   Where could a carer go for dietary advice for a child who has feeding difficulties?
14   What do understand by 'finger feeding'?
15   What safety procedures should you follow at mealtimes for toddlers?

KEY WORDS AND TERMS

You need to know what these words and phrases mean. Go back through the chapter and find out.

eating habits   food refusal
finger feeding   negative response
food and emotion/power

---

6 INFLUENCES ON FOOD AND DIET

> **This chapter covers:**
> ■ School meals
> ■ The food industry and the media
> ■ Poverty
> ■ Food allergies and intolerances

School meals

Cooked school meals were first introduced in 1906 with the aim of improving the nutritional status of those who were poor. To begin with the meals were supplied for just three days a week and often only during winter. In the 1940s, cooked school meals became available as a right for any child who wanted one. This meal was intended to be a child's main meal of the day and was meant to provide one-third of the daily requirements of protein, energy and some vitamins and minerals. The price of these meals was strictly controlled. In addition, free milk was available for all school children.

However, various Education Acts have since brought about major changes in the legislation (laws) governing school meals:

■ In 1980, national nutritional standards and price controls were abolished.
■ Also in 1980, free school milk for all children was withdrawn, although some primary schools continue to purchase milk at subsidised prices.
■ In 1986, schools had to put the supply of meal services out to competitive tender.
■ In 1988, many children lost their eligibility for free meals.
■ Also in 1988, some payments were replaced by direct cash sums to families, which might or might not be spent on food.
■ In 1990, LEAs (local education authorities) were only required to provide meals for children entitled to free dinners and to provide a place for children to eat packed lunches.
■ In 2002, voluntary guidelines were introduced to improve the nutritional content of school meals. School were once again required to provide 'paid lunches' where parents request them.
■ In 2005, the School Meals Review Panel proposed radical changes to the quality and nutritional value of food served and consumed in school.

■ In September 2009, the New School Food Standards became fully phased in.

NEW SCHOOL FOOD STANDARDS

Food provided in schools by local authorities must meet these minimum nutritional standards, which aim to ensure that children are given a balanced, healthy diet.

Under the standards, some foods must be made available:

■ High-quality meat, poultry and oily fish must be regularly available.
■ No less than two portions of fruit and vegetables with every meal – at least one should be vegetables or salad, and at least one should be fruit.
■ Bread with no added fat or oil must be available daily.
■ Other cereals and potatoes must be regularly available.

Some foods must be restricted:

■ Deep-fried food (including chips and battered products) limited to no more than two portions per week.
■ Condiments such as mayonnaise and ketchup can only be served in individual portions of less than 10 g or 1 tsp.
■ Foods including burgers, sausages, pasties and any other shaped or coated meat products cannot be provided any more frequently than once a fortnight, and they must meet the standards for minimum meat content. They may not contain any offal.

Certain foods are not permitted at all:

■ Fizzy drinks, crisps, chocolate and other confectioneries are not allowed within school meals or vending machines.
■ Salt must not be provided on tables or at the service counter.

In recent years there have been a number of health education campaigns relevant to children's nutrition, notably:

■ The '5-A-DAY' programme. This promotes eating five pieces of fresh fruit and vegetables each day. Thanks to the School Fruit and Vegetable Scheme all children aged 4 to 6 who attend an LEA-maintained school are entitled to receive one free piece of fruit or vegetable each day they attend. This follows the National Diet and Nutrition Survey of June 2000, which found that despite the recommendations to eat five portions of fruit and vegetables daily:
  - Children ate on average two portions of fruit and vegetables daily.
  - The consumption of fruit and vegetables has *fallen* since 1983.
  - One in five children eat no fruit in a week.
  - Children in low-income groups are 50 per cent less likely to eat fruit and vegetables.

- Even those children who do eat fruit and vegetables eat less than one portion of each a day.
- Diets of school children are heavily dependent on foods that are rich in fat, sugar and salt.
- Nearly 70 per cent of children between 2 and 12 years old eat biscuits, sweets or chocolate at least once a day.

■ The Water is Cool in School campaign. This has been introduced to improve the access to fresh drinking water in all schools.

■ The Birth to Five guide. A free booklet given to new parents, which introduces child health, safety and nutrition in the early years.

■ Change4Life Campaign. A campaign to encourage and support families to make small changes to eat well, move more and live longer. Families can join at www.nhs.uk/Change4Life. They will then receive a welcome pack. The government's nutrition site (www.eatwell.gov.uk) also gives regularly updated advice on all aspects of nutrition for everyone, from babies to adults.

HEALTHY SCHOOLS PROGRAMME

The White Paper 'Excellence in Schools' (part of 'Our Healthier Nation') proposed an initiative, jointly funded by the Departments of Health and Education, for all schools to aim for 'Healthy Schools' status. The programme was launched in 1999 and still runs today. To achieve this status, schools using a whole-school approach have to reach National Standards set for criteria and levels of achievement in health work. Core themes include PSHE, healthy eating, physical activity and emotional wellbeing. Nationally, 97 per cent of schools are involved in the programme. Over 70 per cent of these have achieved Healthy School status. The government reports that, 'This translates to around 4 million children and young people currently enjoying the benefits of attending a Healthy School.' Visit www.healthyschools.gov.uk/ for further details.

PACKED LUNCHES – THE ALTERNATIVE TO SCHOOL MEALS

The appeal for many carers of providing a healthy midday meal for their child may be offset by the uncertainty that there is no guarantee that the child will eat the contents of his lunchbox. In a busy family packed lunches can be time consuming to buy for, plan and prepare. Frequently, the meal is of cold food and this is an important consideration when it is the midday meal for a young child during winter. There is also a tendency to provide only food that the child is familiar with and likes, limiting the experience of different food. Due to the increasing popularity of packed lunches, the Food Standards Agency and the School Food Trust have produced tips and suggestions for parents and carers. (Visit www.food.gov.uk/news/newsarchive/2004/sep/toplunchboxtips and www.schoolfoodtrust.org.uk/content.asp?Contentid=505.)

Providing a balanced, exciting packed lunch with variety is a challenge. Studies tell us that children prefer their lunchboxes to contain:
■ strong tastes
■ hard, crispy textures
■ items at room temperature or frozen
■ interesting shapes for the food or its container
■ 'finger foods' of bite size.

(d) Look for hidden sugars in any bought foods you are considering.

(e) Remember the energy needs of a 6 year old.

(f) Ensure that the foods you choose transport well.

2 Plan an alternative week's lunches for a child who is vegetarian, using the same criteria as in Activity 1. What sources of iron and B-group vitamins would you choose?

3 Cost both sets of lunches and compare with the prices of traditional or cafeteria dinners at your placement.

4 Which lunches (school meals or packed lunches) do you consider best meet the child's nutritional needs?

REMEMBER!

■ Food may remain in lunch boxes for long periods, increasing the risk of bacterial food poisoning.

■ Prepare any sandwiches or rolls at the last minute, or make and freeze in batches.

■ Use insulated cool bags for transport.

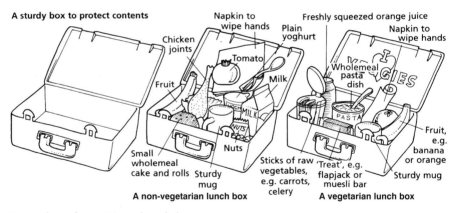

Examples of nutritious lunch boxes

Activity

Design a healthy eating campaign for an infant school, linking classroom learning to encouraging healthier lunchtime choices:

1 Include information about how to choose healthier food and drinks – perhaps colour-coded menus or stars for foods you wish to promote.

2 Think about how you could involve parents or carers in the campaign. Perhaps you could hold a 'tasting' evening of foods from the current menu.

3 Think about how you could celebrate cultural diversity.

BSE/VCJD

New variant Creitzfeld-Jacob disease (vCJD) appears to be linked to eating meat from cows infected with BSE (bovine spongiform encephalopathy, more commonly known as 'mad cow disease'). In vCJD (the human form of BSE), a normally harmless protein called a prion, present in many different human body tissues, has been found to change shape in the brain. It becomes a lethal, disease-causing agent, starting a chain reaction leading to the eventual destruction of the brain. There are strict controls in place in the UK and throughout Europe to protect people from possible exposure to BSE, including the removal from the food chain of the parts of cattle most likely to be affected. The Food Standards Agency monitors these controls and publicises any breaches, as well as the actions taken to avoid further failures.

The food industry and the media

Besides home and school, there are many other influences on children's eating habits, and they are becoming increasingly sophisticated. They can be obvious, such as the popular birthday party facilities at fast-food restaurants. Children keen to be the same as their peers can put strong pressure on parents and carers to hold such parties.

There are other, more subtle influences of which we may be unaware. For example, displays in supermarkets and the placing of sweets, crisps, etc. on the shelves can be very tempting for toddlers, even more so if these items are placed at checkouts where a fraught parent may be queuing to pay, accompanied by a bored child who wants the sweets and chocolates on display.

Packaging, advertisements and the images they promote frequently portray ideas of health, success and happiness – usually in stable, traditional family settings with highly-involved fathers. Breakfasts always seem to be civilised with families sitting around tables with plenty of time, and with everyone even-tempered!

Cans of soft drinks often promote images of amazing athletic or sporting success. Some brands of foods offer reasons for parents and carers to buy them again, for example free games, gifts or series of cards to collect may be included, or offers of reduced prices on future purchases. All of these make it difficult for parents and carers to make decisions solely for nutritional reasons. In 2007, steps to help combat this were taken when 'junk food' adverts were banned from television when programmes aimed at children aged 4 to 9 years old are being shown. The new rule applies to food and drinks high in fat, salt or sugar.

Supermarket checkout

In addition, nutritional information included on packaging can be confusing and technical, for example glucose, fructose, sucrose are all basically sugars – but which is 'best'?

REMEMBER!

When shopping, various influences can affect your decisions on what to puchase:
- ■ price
- ■ taste
- ■ image – television, packaging, magazines
- ■ nutritional value.

Poverty

Families are primarily responsible for ensuring their children are well fed with nutritious food to promote healthy development, but school meals make an important contribution to the daily diet of children in the UK. Children whose parents are in receipt of income support or income-based jobseeker's allowance are entitled to free school meals. Previously families who received family income supplement were also entitled. When this benefit was changed, entitlement to free school meals was withdrawn for working families. A notional amount was included in family credit rates to compensate for the loss of free school meals, but the tendency is for this to be swallowed up in general household expenditure.

Sustain (formerly the National Food Alliance and the SAFE Alliance) has produced evidence of high food poverty among children from low income families, in the UK. Their findings show children going without food for long periods, arriving at school hungry and making very unhealthy food choices. Children were found to be often overweight or underweight. Not being able to waste food was a major issue for many mothers, buying what they knew children would eat, rather than high value nutritional foods, in order to avoid waste. Providing meals during school holidays added pressure to low-income families.

The Government's 'Diets of British Schoolchildren', published in 1989, reported that children from low-income families:

■ depend on cheap food for calories, primarily chips, cakes and biscuits, at the expense of healthier and more expensive foods, such as fruit, vegetables and lean meat

■ have low intakes of folate and vitamins A and C.

School meals continue to contribute between 30–40 per cent of a child's daily energy intake, the higher proportion among low-income families. Children receiving free school meals are particularly dependent on these meals for their daily intake of vitamin C. For many children the school dinner is the main meal of the day – in 1999 a Local Authority Caterers Association survey found that 22 per cent of parents rely on a school meal to provide a balanced diet.

In addition, worrying information from the Child Poverty Action Group's (CPAG) 2000 campaign for free school meals states that:

■ one in three school children in the UK live in poverty, yet only one in five are currently eligible for a free school meal

■ 20 per cent of children entitled to free school meals do not take them; this is thought to be related to the stigma attached

■ 1 million children living in poverty do not get a free school meal

■ the average amount spent on a school meal is £1.28

■ 10 per cent of children are deterred from taking school meals by the cost

■ school meals are the only hot meal received by one in four children.

In evidence to the government on its enquiry into school meals, CPAG stated:

■ Benefits levels fall short of the amount needed to maintain adequate living standards. Research found that families cut back on money spent on food, both in quantity and quality, to meet unexpected expenses.

■ Stigma associated with selection for free school meals was a factor in meals not being taken – in some schools children stand in separate queues, while in cash cafeterias 'cashless' children are readily identified, and pupils report bullying when identified as having free meals. In some areas as many as 40 per cent of school children entitled to free meals do not take them up.

■ Schools should be given clear guidance on what prices are reasonable for school meals.

BREAKFAST CLUBS

Breakfast is acknowledged to be the most important meal of the day. It gives a child the best possible preparation for school. However, figures suggest that nationally 1 in 10 children, rising to 1 in 3 in London, do not have breakfast. As a result breakfast clubs, which provide cheap, nutritionally sound, meals before school, have developed. They currently provide an early meal to about 25 000 children in the UK. These have arisen especially in areas of social deprivation and where working parents need 'out of schools' provision. Studies have shown the benfit of these clubs for children in many areas, including improved academic performance and concentration, reduced truancy levels and a wide range of health benefits.

Clubs can be based in a variety of settings from schools to community centres and may support a number of local schools. However they must fulfil the legal requirements covering the following:
■ the relevant health and safety regulations for premises, equipment, the serving and storage of food, and disposal of waste
■ insurance for public and employer liability, including injury to children and other involved adults
■ child:adult ratios
■ staff qualifications and police checks.
Funding is from a variety of sources, including the general school budget, charities, and initiatives from the Department for Children, Schools and Families. The sources are not constant and there is ongoing pressure to raise money to continue the clubs. There are suggestions that many clubs shut down within a year of starting up, possibly due to financial and staffing difficulties.

CHEAP SOURCES OF ENERGY AND NUTRIENTS

■ Energy: lard, margarine, vegetable oil, white bread, old (not new) potatoes, pasta, breakfast cereals.
■ Protein: liver, eggs, baked beans, cheese, milk, rice, chicken.
■ Carbohydrate: sugar, white bread, potatoes, pasta, biscuits, ice-cream.
■ Iron: liver, fortified breakfast cereals, wholemeal bread.
■ Vitamin A: liver, carrots, margarine, eggs, milk, cheese.
■ Thiamin: fortified breakfast cereals, old (not new) potatoes, wholemeal bread, pork, liver, bacon, ham.
■ Riboflavin: liver, breakfast cereals, bread (white and brown).

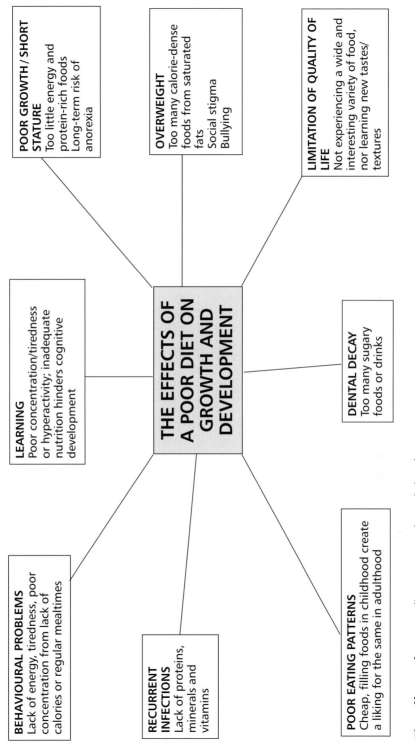

POOR GROWTH / SHORT STATURE
Too little energy and protein-rich foods
Long-term risk of anorexia

OVERWEIGHT
Too many calorie-dense foods from saturated fats
Social stigma
Bullying

LIMITATION OF QUALITY OF LIFE
Not experiencing a wide and interesting variety of food, nor learning new tastes/textures

LEARNING
Poor concentration/tiredness or hyperactivity; inadequate nutrition hinders cognitive development

THE EFFECTS OF A POOR DIET ON GROWTH AND DEVELOPMENT

DENTAL DECAY
Too many sugary foods or drinks

BEHAVIOURAL PROBLEMS
Lack of energy, tiredness, poor concentration from lack of calories or regular mealtimes

RECURRENT INFECTIONS
Lack of proteins, minerals and vitamins

POOR EATING PATTERNS
Cheap, filling foods in childhood create a liking for the same in adulthood

The effects of a poor diet on growth and development

- Niacin: liver, breakfast cereals, white bread, old (not new) potatoes, chicken.
- Vitamin C: fruit juice, oranges, old (not new) potatoes, tomatoes.
- Vitamin D: margarine, fatty fish, eggs, liver.
- Fibre: dried beans, wholemeal bread, baked beans.

Activity

1 Plan a week's basic shopping for a family of four – two adults (the father is unemployed) and two children, aged 5 and 7 (receiving free school meals):
   - Include staples such as bread, milk, margarine and the ingredients for three daily meals.
   - Ensure your basket will meet the nutritional needs of the family.
   - Include fresh fruit and vegetables.
   - Cost should include at least three main meat meals.
2 Assess the total spending.
3 Research the financial benefits a family like this would receive. Subtract the cost of your week's shopping and indicate how much would remain for other expenses.

REMEMBER!

Extra costs are incurred in cooking and preparation.

Food allergies and intolerances

- An **allergy** is the body's rejection of a food.
- An **intolerance** is the body's inability to digest or absorb a specific food. Many symptoms have been blamed on what is popularly, but inaccurately, called food allergy. Two in ten people in the population believe they are allergic to certain foods, but in reality fewer than 10 per cent of those can be proved medically. Only about 1–2 per cent of the population have proveable reactions to food, and only a minority of these reactions are true allergies. It is essential that accurate diagnosis is made before foods are withdrawn from a child's diet, because severe dietary modification can result in malnutrition. Frequently, symptoms assumed to be related to food are in fact caused by a totally different trigger, such as an infection or stress.

FOODS PROVOKING ADVERSE REACTIONS

The most common foods that provoke reactions are milk, egg, fish and shellfish, nuts and peanuts, soya, pork, bacon, texturised meat substitutes (see TVP on Proteins chart, page 17), food additives, chocolate, coffee, tea, citrus fruit and strawberries.

SAFE PRACTICE

Always liaise with parents and carers so you are aware of any foods that should not be given to a child. Remember, too, that nuts are used in a variety of different foods and that their presence may not always be obvious.

WHAT IS AN ADVERSE REACTION TO FOOD?

An adverse reaction may simply be a result of dislike of a food, or it may be the result of a food allergy or of food poisoning.
- Food dislike
  - Psychological factors, for example the food may be associated with unpleasant feelings/occasions.
  - Temporary intolerance: physical signs may include vomiting, diarrhoea, transient rashes.
  - Food avoidance: tastes or textures may be unacceptable to the child, for example toddlers sometimes reject lumpy food for long periods.
- Food allergy, causing a severe body response, including:
  - swelling of the mucous membranes, leading to breathing difficulties
  - wheeziness
  - severe rashes
  - vomiting and diarrhoea
  - faltering growth
  - symptoms worse when food eaten again
  - often not 'grown out of'.
- Food poisoning, caused by the body's response to contaminated food, usually short-lived, but symptoms may be acute, including diarrhoea, vomiting and abdominal pain.

It is important to decide what is the cause of any adverse response to a certain meal or food.

Anaphylaxis
Anaphylaxis is an extreme, life-threatening allergic reaction, which can occur rarely. Triggers for this are commonly nuts, eggs, fish, especially shellfish, bee and wasp stings, and occasionally some antibiotic medicines. Children should wear identification bracelets if they are known to have this reaction.

Symptoms develop rapidly, starting with:
- rash and tingling of the skin
- swelling of the face and throat, leading to airway restriction
- increasing difficulty in breathing
- shock and death.

This is a major emergency requiring an immediate response. Seek help and call an ambulance.

Children who have had a diagnosed episode of anaphylaxis will have two pre-loaded syringes of adrenalin (EpiPen or Anapen), that should be readily available at all times. Carers, school and nursery staff should all know where they are kept. The fine needle of the syringe is inserted into a fleshy part of the outer arm or thigh and the drug given, when the effect should be immediate. A second dose can be given after five minutes if necessary.

SAFE PRACTICE

In any setting where it is known a child is vulnerable to anaphylaxis, everyone should know:
- exactly what food and drinks the child may and may not have. Even touching a certain food could be enough to make some children ill. All carers must be absolutely clear on the procedures in place to protect a child with an allergy. Sadly, a baby died recently after being given the wrong bottle of milk by a member of staff at a day nursery
- how to recognise the signs of anaphylactic shock in the child
- how to respond to this potentially life-threatening emergency. Individual workers should receive training in giving adrenalin, which may be life saving.

Milk protein allergy

This is rare and can occur at any age. It is thought to affect about 2 per cent of children in the first year of life. It is is usually associated with a family history of allergy, for example asthma, hay fever or eczema. Symptoms include faltering growth, diarrhoea and vomiting, rashes and recurrent respiratory infections. Treatment requires specialist advice. Soya milk and goat's milks have shown similar adverse responses to cow's milks, and it is now advised that babies, following diagnosis, are fed a special milk formula made from **hydrolysed protein** and obtained on a prescription from a doctor. Check when using proprietor's weaning foods that they do not contain milk products.

Lactose intolerance

Lactose is the natural sugar found in milk and foods containing milk. Intolerance occurs when a baby lacks lactase, which is an enzyme needed to break down lactose into glucose for digestion. The baby will have diarrhoea, abdominal pain and frothy stools. Following diagnosis a special formula feed will be required. Children usually 'grow out' of this intolerance.

Hyperactivity

Some children adopt abnormally active behaviour – they are restless, have poor concentration and need very little sleep. Occasionally this can be traced to a reaction to food or a food additive.

The prime causes are thought to be **tartrazine**, an orange colouring used in squashes and sweets, and benzoic acid, a **preservative**. Colourings used in foods are indicated on products as **E numbers** from 100–180, and preservatives with E numbers 200–283 (see Additives, Chapter 9, pages 156–7).

Often other factors need to be taken into account before deciding that certain behaviour is caused by a food or an additive. The personality of the child, family tensions resulting from difficult or pre-term births, stressful childhood incidents, such as family breakdown, disruptions in routine and the 'normal' negativity of many 2 year olds, can all produce behaviour described as hyperactivity. Medical opinion is severely divided as to the true incidence of behaviour difficulties, which are actually due to food additives. So, as with any other intolerance, careful diagnosis is essential before a severely restricting diet is applied to a young child.

Children often outgrow food intolerances and it is the usual practice for excluded foods to be reintroduced periodically under appropriate medical supervision. Certainly, no child should stay on a milk-free diet for longer than necessary. As well as the energy value of milk, calcium intake is important and can be affected.

TESTING FOR ALLERGIES AND INTOLERANCES

As intolerance and food dislike need different management from allergy it is necessary to try and discover the cause of the problem, in order that the food or 'allergen' can be excluded from the diet. In addition to weighing and examining the child, the family doctor will take a full and detailed history of the worrying signs, and symptoms, together with information from the family of any history of allergies. The doctor may refer the child to a paediatrician, nutritionist or specialist allergy clinic where a variety of further investigations and tests may be ordered. The most common tests are described below.

Skin prick test

A small needle introduces the allergen into the skin. Within 15–20 minutes the skin around the area will become itchy and red with swelling if there is an allergic response.

Blood tests

Over 400 different allergens can be tested for in this way, including food sources. Samples are taken to measure specific immunoglobulin E antibodies (IgE) to various environmental and food allergies. The response is graded 0–6, depending on the level of IgE in the blood.

Patch test

This is primarily used for allergens caused by direct contact and less by foods. Various allergens are taped on to the skin for 48 hours and the skin is watched for response, as in the skin prick test.

Challenge test

The specific test for food allergy challenge is called the 'double-blind placebo food challenge'. In this test the suspected cause is hidden in a capsule or soup and given under careful supervision. This test, although the most accurate, is time consuming and must be undertaken in hospital where resuscitation equipment is available, in case of anaphylaxis.

Alternative tests

There are many other alternative tests available, but care should be taken with young children that these have been suitably scrutinised and assessed for accuracy before restricting a child's diet.

PREVENTION OF ALLERGY

For babies expected in families where parents or siblings have a history of severe allergy the additional advice is as follows:
- The pregnant mother should avoid smoking and highly allergenic foods in the last half of her pregnancy.
- She should aim to exclusively breast-feed her baby and continue not to eat allergenic foods while breast-feeding. If breast-feeding is not possible, special hypoallergenic formula milk may be advised.
- Weaning should be delayed until the baby is 6 months of age and then restricted initially to lamb, chicken, rice, sweet potatoes, carrots and pears.
- Foods to be avoided up to 1 year of age are milk – cow and goat – wheat, fish, soya and citrus fruits.
- Ground nuts should only introduced, with care, from 3 years of age.
- Food labels must be scrutinised to monitor contents, particularly watching for hidden nuts, additives and preservatives that may provoke allergic response.

QUICK CHECK

1 Look at the following list. Do these outside influences affect children's nutrition in your placement?
   (a) Is there a school 'tuck shop'?
   (b) How near to the school gates can parents and carers or children buy sweets?
   (c) Does the ice-cream van regularly wait outside the playground?
   (d) Is there a sweets policy in the school?
2 How could you provide interesting, balanced and varied diets from the 'cheap' sources of nutrients listed on page 100?
3 What are the effects of poor diet on the total growth and development of a child?
4 What are the differences between:
   (a) food dislike
   (b) food allergy
   (c) food poisoning?
5 Describe the symptoms of lactose intolerance.
6 What factors, other than the eating of specific food colourings, might cause a child to be labelled 'hyperactive'?
7 What nutritional advice, regarding infant feeding, could you give an expectant mother with a family history of allergy and intolerance?
8 How may changes in government legislation have affected the nutritional content of school meals?
9 What suggestions could you make to a parent or carer about the safe packaging of packed lunches?
10 Which additives/preservatives may be linked to hyperactivity in children?
11 Describe the life-threatening symptoms of true allergy.
12 List three cheap sources of high biological value (HBV) protein.
13 What are the social and emotional benefits of children eating school dinners?
14 Argue the case for packed lunches versus school dinners.
15 What could be the effects of a poor diet on a child's cognitive development?

KEY WORDS AND TERMS

You need to know what these words and phrases mean. Go back through the chapter and find out.

allergy	hyperactivity
benefits	intolerance
challenge test	lactose intolerance
'double-blind' trial	milk protein allergy
enzyme	patch test
hydrolysed protein	tartrazine

7 *DISORDERS REQUIRING SPECIAL DIETS*

This chapter covers:
■ **Special diets**
  – coeliac condition
  – cystic fibrosis
  – insulin-dependent diabetes
  – phenylketonuria

Whenever essential nutrients cannot be absorbed or used by the child's body, or there is particular intolerance to certain foods, that child's growth, health and development are likely to be affected in some way. The effects on the child depend on the nature of the condition, but typically there may be:
■ poor growth (both weight and height)
■ delayed learning and physical development
■ recurrent health problems, such as coughs and colds, chest infections and anaemia
■ social and emotional difficulties.

Children with disorders, such as those set out in this chapter, may spend periods of time in hospital separated from family, friends and peers, perhaps undergoing unpleasant tests and treatment, and missing valuable time at nursery or school. Many disorders, allergies and intolerances can be alleviated by modern treatment and special diet, so that, as far as possible, normal growth and development takes place.

Special diets

Special diets are worked out by the doctor and dietician according to the individual needs of the child. Food preferences, as well as cultural and religious dietary traditions, will be respected. Adjustments to the diet will be made from time to time, especially when nutritional needs alter as the child grows. A hospital or community dietician supervises the diet, and provides help and advice for parents and carers. Nursery and school staff, nannies and childminders, require a full understanding of why a child is on a special diet, and what foods the child can and cannot eat. They must also keep a record of the diet and medicines a child may be receiving. So close liaison and co-operation with parents or carers is essential. Kitchen and canteen staff also require details of special diets they need to prepare.

A child maintaining a life-long diet will need significant support during her nursery and school days. Simple and consistent explanations as to why certain foods are not allowed are essential for young children. As they get older, they will become expert at knowing what is or is not permitted, gradually adapting and managing easily, and making the link between feeling well and keeping to the diet. Careful supervision at mealtimes is initially necessary to ensure a child does not swap her diet foods with a friend's food. Some diets may have to be eaten at regular times in order to maintain good health. This could cause problems for children with diabetes if, for example, there is a long wait in the queue for school dinner, or a toddler decides to assert independence by refusing to eat.

To avoid difficulties or misunderstandings at parties, or during outings, nursery and school staff should discuss relevant dietary needs beforehand with parents or carers.

The hospital specialist and family doctor will regularly assess the child's health and development. Voluntary and self-help organisations for particular disorders offer advice and support for children and their families.

REMEMBER!

■ Knowledge of the long-term implications for a child of failure to keep to the special diet is important for all carers.
■ Always discuss a child's particular dietary needs with your supervisor.

Activity
Research the following questions and write up your findings:
1 Is there a child in your nursery or school who must follow a special diet?
2 What are the reasons for the diet and which foods are restricted?
3 Where is the record of the child's diet kept? Who has access to it?
4 Are meal timings important for the child?

Disorders requiring special diets

COELIAC CONDITION

Coeliac condition is a disorder of the small intestine caused by intolerance to gluten. It often occurs in families and is usually detected in infancy or childhood. Gluten, a protein found in wheat, barley, rye and oats, damages the lining of the small intestine resulting in poor absorption of essential nutrients. Symptoms usually start within a few months of food containing gluten being introduced during the weaning process. They include: loose, bulky, greasy, foul-smelling stools (due to poor absorption of fat), which are difficult to flush away; faltering growth (failure to thrive) and developmental delay; poor appetite and anaemia; lethargy and irritability. There is also muscle wasting, especially of the buttocks, and a distended stomach (see illustration below). A special blood test and an intestinal biopsy will confirm the diagnosis.

Coeliac condition is permanent, but a child will quickly respond once he is eating a gluten-free diet, and should thrive and remain healthy. The diet is for life and must be strictly maintained. If the diet lapses the symptoms will reappear. Supplements of vitamin D, folic acid and iron are usually prescribed.

Offering gluten-free weaning cereals and foods to all infants in the initial stages of weaning may reduce the risk of coeliac condition. Typically, rice cereal is offered to babies at the beginning of weaning. Gluten-free flours, breads and plain biscuits can be obtained on prescription from the family doctor, and a range of gluten-free foods is available in supermarkets and many health-food shops. They are usually identified on the nutritional

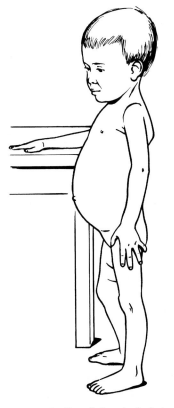

A child with coeliac disease – note the distended abdomen and wasted buttocks

Coeliac UK cross-grained symbol, which indicates that food is gluten-free

label by the words 'gluten free' with a 'tick' sign beside them, or by the words 'suitable for a gluten-free diet'. Some gluten-free foods will display the cross-grained symbol, used under licence from Coeliac UK (www.coeliac.org.uk), a charity which aims to improve the lives of people with coeliac condition.

Suitable and unsuitable foods for children with coeliac condition
Most plainly prepared, natural foods (apart from those containing wheat, barley, rye and oats) can be eaten. Home-cooked foods are ideal, although may be more costly and more time consuming to prepare than bought foods. Cereals containing gluten, especially wheat flour, are commonly used as binders, fillers and coatings in processed foods such as meat and fish products, so vigilance is necessary when buying foods. Coeliac UK produces regularly updated lists of gluten-free manufactured products. If a product is not on the list it should not be included in a child's diet. Make sure your work setting has the most recent updated list. A hospital or community dietician will advise a child and carers on what constitutes a gluten-free diet and offer follow-up help and guidance.

Some foods that do not contain gluten and can be eaten include:
- fruit and vegetables (fresh, raw, dried, frozen and tinned)
- pure fruit and vegetable juices
- milk, cream, yoghurt, unprocessed cheese, eggs, fats and oils
- fresh meat, poultry and fish
- rice (all types), tapioca, maize and buckwheat
- gluten-free flours: potato, rice, soya and corn, also arrowroot
- gluten-free bread, cakes and biscuits
- nuts (but whole or broken nuts must never be given to children under 5 years).

Some foods that contain gluten and cannot be eaten include:
- breads, cakes and biscuits made with non gluten-free flours
- breakfast cereals such as Weetabix and Shredded Wheat
- coated or processed foods such as fish fingers, chicken nuggets, sausages, burgers and processed cheeses, also any other food containing cereal binders and fillers, food starches and food stabilisers
- tinned and packet soups, bottled sauces and salad creams
- instant whips, mousses and similar desserts, ice-cream.

REMEMBER!

- The composition of manufactured and processed foods changes from time to time. Always take Coeliac UK's up-to-date list with you when shopping to check the contents of food against the labelling.
- Carefully check the labels of foods you are not sure of, and encourage parents and other carers to do the same. Many manufactured baby foods, processed meat products and soups contain 'hidden' gluten in the form of fillers, binders and coatings.

Helping a young child with coeliac condition and the family

Useful ways of managing a young child's nutrition within the family can include the following:

- use gluten-free flours for all family cooking purposes
- offer the same food to all the family and visitors
- accept invitations, but make sure the child takes his own gluten-free food with him, or that the adults who will be caring for him know of, and can provide for, his dietary needs
- always tell a child why certain foods are not allowed and link your explanations to the fact that he is remaining healthy
- do not blame every minor stomach upset on the child's 'condition'
- avoid routine discussion about a child's symptoms or his diet in front of him.

Ongoing management

All those involved in the child's care, including nursery and school staff and dinner supervisors, must know what foods are acceptable. Special awareness is necessary: for those organising parties, nursery or school trips and outings; when staff change at dinner times; and when a child is unwell. A matter-of-fact approach to coeliac condition is helpful, coupled with an understanding that the condition is for life.

Activity

1 Obtain a current copy of Coeliac UK's list of gluten-free products. From the list, identify popular breakfast cereals that *can* and *cannot* be offered to children with coeliac condition.

2 (a) Visit a supermarket, taking the gluten-free list with you. Check at least 15 foods on the list, looking for information stating that each product is gluten free.

  (b) Could you find 15 foods?

  (c) How easy or difficult was it to find reference to gluten on the nutritional labels?

3 How time-consuming was this exercise?

CYSTIC FIBROSIS

Cystic fibrosis is a genetically inherited, life-threatening condition affecting 1 in 2500 children. Many children with cystic fibrosis used to die in childhood or their early teens from pneumonia, but with better knowledge of the disorder and advances in treatment and dietary management, they are now surviving well into adulthood. Heart and lung transplants are offering a cure to some people. The faulty gene responsible for cystic fibrosis can be identified during pregnancy and research aimed at replacing it continues.

Cystic fibrosis particularly affects the respiratory and digestive systems. Symptoms occur in the first few months of life. Large quantities of thick, sticky mucus form in the lungs and the pancreatic ducts. Damage to the lungs from repeated coughs, colds and chronic chest infections is the most serious worry. Blockage of the pancreatic ducts prevents enzymes, particularly pancreatin, from passing into the intestines. Consequently, nutrients, especially fats and protein, cannot be absorbed and utilised by the body. Instead, they are excreted in the stools, which are bulky, greasy and unpleasantly smelly. Complications, such as chest infections, abdominal pain and distension, and vomiting during bouts of coughing are common, causing loss of appetite and consequent poor energy intake, while the extra effort of breathing results in higher energy expenditure. Examination of the child's sweat shows an abnormally high sodium chloride (salt) content due to malfunctioning of the sweat glands. This is a typical diagnostic sign of cystic fibrosis.

Caring for children with cystic fibrosis

Care and treatment for children with cystic fibrosis aims to stabilise the condition by: maintaining good nutrition; physiotherapy and exercises; offering current childhood immunisations; and good personal and environmental hygiene routines.

Nutritional intake for a child with cystic fibrosis

Special care and attention to nutritional intake for a child with cystic fibrosis is essential. Good nutrition is vital to ensure, and maintain, proper growth and development, and reduce the risk of respiratory infections. A well-balanced high protein, high calorie diet is generally recommended. This means encouraging a child to eat foods rich in fat and sugar, although calorie intake will be matched to a child's individual growth and energy needs, and the level of tolerated fat taken into account. It may be difficult for a child to take in the required level of calories during periods of infection when loss of appetite is common, so **enteral nutrition** (see Chapter 8, pages 142–3) may be necessary at these times.

Pancreatic enzyme replacement, to aid the absorption of fat, must be taken with every meal and whenever a fatty snack or drink is given. It is not necessary if just a fruit snack is eaten. With enzyme replacement fat absorption can rise to 80–90 per cent of normal.

Dietary principles include:
- at least three regular meals plus snacks every day
- foods rich in fat and sugar, for example
  - whole milk and milky drinks and sauces, milk puddings, steamed and sponge puddings, custard made with milk, full-fat cheese and yoghurt, butter, ice-cream and fried food, including chips
  - jams, biscuits, cakes, tinned fruit in syrup
  - starchy carbohydrates such as bread, potatoes, rice, pasta
  - protein foods such as meat, poultry, fish (or alternatives)
  - additional special high energy and protein foods such as milk shakes and glucose drinks if the child fails to grow and gain weight
- daily fat-soluble vitamins A, D, E and K.

REMEMBER!

Even with effective enzyme replacement, food absorption is not perfect so the quality of the diet is important. Filling up on 'junk' foods or foods with only limited nutritional content is not an option.

Very young children

Infants and toddlers with cystic fibrosis are at risk of faltering growth (see Chapter 8, pages 130–4). Breast milk is very beneficial to all babies but for those with cystic fibrosis it is a most valuable source of energy because it contains a particular fat-digesting enzyme (lipase), which splits fatty acids to form energy. Breast feeds should be offered frequently. Babies can thrive satisfactorily on standard formula milks but some may require a special high-energy formula. Daily pancreatic enzyme is given to all babies and toddlers with cystic fibrosis, and can be mixed with a little water, milk or fruit purée. High calorie and sodium (salt) supplements are usually prescribed.

Weaning can begin at the usual time of 6 months, but a particularly hungry baby may need solids from 3 months. Carers should follow normal weaning processes and practices, but add extra butter and milk to foods. The dose of pancreatic enzyme will need adjusting as the amount of food increases.

Because diet is so important to the health of the child, carers may be upset if a toddler goes through a phase of food fads and food refusal. Adults should remain calm, consistent and encouraging. Remember, a toddler has a small stomach so offer small, regular meals. If a food is refused, try and offer a nutrient-dense, acceptable alternative (see Nutrition for toddlers, Chapter 5, pages 84–7).

REMEMBER!

Never put pancreatic enzyme into a baby's bottle or mix it with a child's food.

School children

When a child with cystic fibrosis eats away from home, carers must know:
- her special nutritional needs
- that pancreatic enzyme must be taken at each meal or with each fatty snack
- where her medicines will be stored and that there are adequate supplies
- how her dietary choice and intake will be monitored
- that extra food will be needed if she takes part in physical activity
- that salt supplement will be necessary in very hot weather or after strenuous activity.

REMEMBER!

A child may feel embarrassed at needing medication at every meal. Try to ensure that she has privacy.

It is always important to achieve the right balance between pancreatic enzyme replacement and calorie intake. Parents may be concerned about the high fat and sugar content of the diet. They need to be reassured with careful explanations and support from the doctor, nutritionist and other professional carers. The Cystic Fibrosis Trust (www.cftrust.org.uk), a voluntary organisation, also provides support, advice and information for children and their families.

Physiotherapy and physical exercise

Physiotherapy is carried out several times a day to help the child to cough up mucus and keep her lungs clear and working properly. Outdoor physical activity, swimming and PE, blowing games and music and movement are ideal exercises for a child with cystic fibrosis.

Activity

A group of 7-year-old children in your class are going on an outing in a few weeks' time and will be taking a picnic lunch with them. Jane, one of the children, has cystic fibrosis. Her parents have asked your advice about suitable foods for Jane to take in her picnic box.

1 What foods and drink would you suggest? Give reasons for your choices.
2 When would Jane need to take her pancreatic enzyme medicine?

TYPE 1 DIABETES

Insulin-dependent Type 1 diabetes usually presents in late childhood but can occur from about the age of 2 years through to adulthood. There is a marked increase in the incidence of children aged 3–5 years with Type 1 diabetes. Type 2 diabetes is non-insulin dependent, presents in middle or old age, and is controlled by diet and oral medication.

Diabetes is a condition affecting carbohydrate metabolism. Normally, the hormone **insulin**, produced by the pancreas, breaks down glucose in the blood and converts it into energy for use by the body. In diabetes there is little or no insulin produced for this conversion and the blood glucose level rises. The kidneys are unable to cope with the excess glucose and it spills over into the urine. Large amounts of urine are produced, depleting the body of water, sodium and potassium. Because the body has no energy from glucose, the child becomes listless and loses weight. If the situation is not noticed the child continues to lose fluids, becoming dehydrated and drowsy. In order to maintain energy levels the body breaks down fat causing ketones in the urine (ketoacidosis) and a pear-drop smell on the breath. This can be very serious, leading to coma and death if medical aid is not urgently sought.

There is no cure for diabetes, but it can be successfully controlled by daily insulin injections and attention to diet. Insulin cannot be given by mouth because it is protein based and would be digested and neutralised in the stomach.

Indications of diabetes in a child include:

- excessive thirst, dry mouth and frequent drinking
- frequent trips to the lavatory, passing large amounts of urine
- bedwetting, especially in a child who was previously dry at night
- loss of appetite and weight loss
- tiredness and lethargy, blurred vision
- urinary infections, genital irritation and thrush infection.

These signs and symptoms develop in a matter of days or weeks. A final diagnosis is made through blood and urine tests.

Nutrition

The aim of nutrition for a child with diabetes is to maintain the blood glucose level within normal range and provide sufficient energy for normal growth, weight and physical exercise. Nutrition for a child with diabetes should be healthy, balanced and varied, high in starchy carbohydrates and fibre, low in sugar and saturated fat. Normal protein intake is allowed. Special diabetic foods are not necessary. They are expensive and usually contain sorbitol, which can cause diarrhoea.

Three main meals and two to three snacks a day, taken at regular times, are recommended. The diet plan, showing the amounts to be eaten, as well as the types of foods allowed, must be available for nursery and school staff, including those preparing meals in kitchens and canteens.

Food choices and intake must include:

■ *at least one* starchy carbohydrate food, for example, bread, potatoes, rice, pasta, cereal, eaten at every meal. Starches take longer to digest than sugars and keep blood glucose levels near normal

■ a good intake of high-fibre cereals, fruit and vegetables (especially oranges and pulses)

■ restricted intake of sugar-rich foods, except in certain circumstances (see below), to prevent too rapid a rise in blood glucose levels. Artificial sweeteners other than sorbitol, can be used on cereals and other foods

■ normal intake of protein from meat, poultry and fish sources and/or vegetable and plant alternatives

■ a limited intake of animal fat. Offer low fat cheeses and grilled foods. Trim the fat from meat and remove the skin from chicken. Semi-skimmed milk can be offered to children over 2 years; skimmed milk for those over 5 years

■ fat-soluble vitamins - they are important nutrients and are usually prescribed as supplements, depending on the overall fat content of the diet.

It is important for Early Years workers to understand that:

■ a child with diabetes should never miss a meal or be kept waiting for a meal. Serve a young child first and allow an older child to go to the head of a school meal queue to avoid waiting

■ a child's dietary routine may mean that snacks (such as a cereal bar or piece of fruit) may need to be eaten in class or during group time

■ sugary foods (quickly absorbed) are necessary to raise a child's blood glucose level quickly (see 'hypo' complication below). Examples of these foods include fizzy drinks and fruit juices, sweets, glucose tablets, chocolate, jam and fruit

■ a sugar snack, such as a small chocolate bar, two biscuits or a glucose drink, should be taken before and during any vigorous activity (swimming, PE, sports) in case the blood sugar level drops. A young child will need reminding to eat her snack. After an activity a child may need to eat some more food

■ regular meal and snack times must be maintained on an outing. Make sure a child has glucose tablets or a sugary drink with her when away from the setting.

Once a child gets to know how her body responds to an 'eating and taking insulin' routine, small amounts of sweets and low fat crisps can be eaten occasionally within the overall diet plan.

Sweets and crisps should be eaten only occasionally

REMEMBER!

■ Failure to maintain a child's proper and regular nutritional intake may result in long-term medical problems, especially of the eyes, skin, kidneys and circulatory system.

■ If a child is hungry on her diet, tell her parents or carers and dietician.

Young children

Young children with diabetes also require regular meals and snacks. Find out from parents their child's likes and dislikes and usual eating routine. Meals should be based around starchy carbohydrates and snacks of fruit, sandwiches and milk. Never force a young child to eat; try and provide an alternative food. All the general principles of feeding toddlers apply, as set out in Chapter 5, pages 84–7.

A young child with diabetes in your nursery needs a sugary food (a biscuit or mini chocolate bar) before a physical activity. Keep a drink of fruit juice to hand in case she needs it during the activity. Be aware of the signs of a 'hypo' complication, as a young child will not be able to tell you how she feels. Ask her parents what the signs are likely to be (see page 120), as they may vary from child to child. Make sure you can distinguish a young child's normal tiredness and behaviour from the signs and symptoms of a 'hypo'.

Recognising hypoglycaemia and hyperglycaemia

It is important to know the signs of hypoglycaemia and hyperglycaemia, and how to care for a child with either complication. Supplies of sugary snacks, such as a carton of sweetened fizzy drink, sugar lumps or glucose tablets, should be always be to hand in the home, nursery room or class room. Insulin must also be available.

Hypoglycaemia

Hypoglycaemia ('a hypo') is the most common short-term complication in diabetes. It happens when the blood glucose level is too low. It occurs suddenly, often before meals. The causes are: too little food (perhaps a missed meal or snack); too much insulin; or excessive exercise without extra glucose or sugar snack. The warning signs include dizziness, sweating, pallor, vagueness and loss of concentration, glazed eyes, sickness, mood changes (becoming angry or aggressive).

The care of the child is the same for all age groups. Quick treatment is needed to reverse the hypoglycaemia so:

■ give a sugary drink (Lucozade, non-diet fizzy drink, glucose tablets or fresh fruit juice). If the child is very drowsy and this is not possible, try rubbing a little jam or glucose gel on to her gums or on the inside of her mouth
■ if the child loses consciousness, place her in the recovery position and get medical help immediately. *Never give an unconsciousness child anything by mouth*
■ once the child recovers, and if her next meal is not due for a while, offer a carbohydrate food such as a sandwich or biscuits and a glass of milk or a piece of fruit.

SAFE PRACTICE

■ A sugar supply should always be readily available, whether the child is indoors or outdoors and whether she is at home or in a care or education setting. Always accompany a child to get her sugar supply if it is not to hand, so that she is not alone if she becomes very unwell and disorientated.
■ Never leave a child alone during a 'hypo' emergency.

Hyperglycaemia

Hyperglycaemia ('a hyper') occurs when the blood sugar level is too high. It occurs slowly.

It is caused by too little insulin, illness or infection. Signs are similar to those before diagnosis of diabetes – thirst, passing large amounts of urine, sleepiness, pear-drop smell to breath. Medical help and insulin injection are urgently needed to prevent unconsciousness.

■ Always inform the parents if their child has either of the above attacks.

■ Children with diabetes should always have with them; sugar supplies; identification card or bracelet; blood glucose testing meter; spare insulin pen (or syringe, needles and dose of insulin).

The Community or Hospital Diabetes Team monitors children with diabetes, and Diabetes UK (www.diabetes.org.uk) provides information, advice and literature for children and their families, and produces a School Pack for teachers.

Activity

You are a nanny caring for three children. One of the children, John, aged 5 years, has recently been diagnosed with diabetes. He is responding well to his insulin and dietary regime. His mother is taking him away for a weekend break to see his grandmother and is anxious that John 'has the right food' while away from home. She has asked you to devise a menu for three meals and three snacks for each of the two days away.
Write out your menu plan based on the dietary principles set out above.

PHENYLKETONURIA

Phenylketonuria (PKU) is genetically inherited and occurs in about 1 in 10 000 births. It is caused by excess of **phenylalanine**, an essential amino acid, which cannot be broken down and absorbed by the body due to the lack of a liver enzyme. Phenylalanine builds up in the bloodstream and causes brain damage and learning delay. There is no cure but early diagnosis and treatment will promote normal development and learning.

All newborn babies in the UK are screened (using the Guthrie test) for this disorder between 6 to 12 days after birth, by which time the baby has had several days of milk feeds. The Guthrie test involves testing a sample of blood from a heel prick for the level of phenylalanine. An abnormally high level confirms the diagnosis. Treatment is a life-long low-phenylalanine diet. The main principles of the diet, which must provide adequate protein for growth, are:

■ special infant formula feed (a small feed of breast milk may be given *after* the formula feed)

■ small amounts of natural protein plus substitute protein formula foods which are available on prescription

■ vitamin and mineral supplements taken with the protein substitute or as a medicine.

A woman with phenylketonuria needs to maintain a low-phenylalanine diet during pregnancy to reduce the risk of harm to her baby.

Babies and young children with phenylketonuria will have regular blood tests. Normal development can be achieved by keeping to the life-long diet – one of the most restrictive of all special diets. It may be possible to relax some dietary rules once brain growth is complete.

As a general rule:

■ high protein foods such as meat, fish, cheese, eggs, pulses and nuts *are not* allowed
■ milk, cereals and potatoes *may be* allowed in small amounts
■ most fruit and vegetables, fats, sugars, jams and honey *are* allowed
■ special bread and flour, biscuits and pasta are available on prescription
■ a carefully formulated list of 'food exchanges' (substituting a food from one list with a food from another list) is usually given to the family, aimed at bringing a little variety and difference into meals.

The National Society for Phenylketonuria (NSPKU) (www.nspku.org) offers help and advice to children and their families, and produces literature and up-to-date food lists.

QUICK CHECK

1 Which professionals are involved in working out special diets for children?
2 Name three factors a doctor or dietician will take into account when planning a special diet for a child.
3 Which particular protein is a child with coeliac condition unable to tolerate?
4 What are the typical signs of coeliac condition?
5 What is the *main* dietary principle in the treatment of coeliac condition?
6 Which two body systems, in particular, are affected by cystic fibrosis?
7 What are the main symptoms of cystic fibrosis?
8 Why does a child with cystic fibrosis require such a high calorie intake?
9 What would lead you to suspect that a child in your care might have diabetes?
10 How would you recognise a 'hypo' complication in a child with diabetes?
11 What emergency care would you give a *conscious* child with diabetes who developed a 'hypo' complication?
12 What items should a child with diabetes carry at all times?
13 Name the blood test used to diagnose phenylketonuria.
14 Name the nutrient that is severely restricted in the diet for a child with phenylketonuria.
15 Name the voluntary organisations for the above four conditions.

KEY WORDS AND TERMS

You need to know what these words and phrases mean. Go back through the chapter and find out.

coeliac condition

cystic fibrosis

gluten

Guthrie test

hyperglycaemia

hypoglycaemia

insulin

insulin-dependent diabetes

pancreatic enzyme

phenylalanine

phenylketonuria

8 COMMON CONDITIONS – DIETARY NEEDS

> **This chapter covers:**
> - Overweight, obesity and underweight
> - Iron-deficiency anaemia
> - Faltering growth
> - Vitamin deficiency disorders
> - Dental caries
> - Constipation
> - Nutrition for an unwell child

Lack of variety in children's nutrition, feeding difficulties, over-consumption of unhealthy foods or deficiency of particular vitamins or minerals, can lead to a number of diet-related conditions. By altering a child's diet and offering support and encouragement to the family it is possible to prevent or reverse many of these conditions.

Overweight, obesity and underweight

- Overweight = 10–20 per cent over ideal weight.
- Obesity = 20 per cent (or more) over ideal weight.

There has been a marked increase in the number of overweight and obese children in the UK (and throughout the developed world) over the last decade. Genetic factors, family lifestyle and special needs that restrict physical activity may increase the risk of unhealthy weight gain in some children. However, most commonly, the cause is a combination of;
- snacking on too many high-calorie foods and drinks
- a decrease in the level of physical activity
- a sedentary lifestyle and too much time spent on non-physical activities.

The result is an imbalance between the number of calories taken into the body (which may not always be excessive) and the number of calories used up by the body in its daily functions and activities. The excess of unused calories is stored as fat. Many attractively packaged energy-dense foods and drinks are marketed to appeal to children and are regularly eaten as snacks or even as replacements for nutritionally balanced meals. Walking, games and sports that burn up calories are being replaced by 'couch potato' activities, such as watching television, using the internet and computer/video games.

Excess body fat puts a child at risk of developing a range of health problems in later life (see Overweight and obesity in adulthood, page 128). Early Years workers, health visitors and family doctors can promote healthy eating habits among young children and offer sensible nutritional advice to families.

OVERWEIGHT AND OBESITY IN INFANCY

An overfed baby will develop extra fat cells, which then continuously demand to be filled. The effects of this may include:

■ delayed motor development (rolling, crawling, walking, climbing, running)
■ mechanical disorders of hips, legs and feet
■ greater risk of accidents
■ recurrent chest infections
■ chafing and soreness where skin surfaces rub together
■ breathlessness
■ greater expectations by adults because baby looks older.
   Possible causes are:
■ over-concentrated bottle-feeds; encouraging baby to finish up bottle when she is clearly satisfied
■ addition of sugar and/or cereal to bottle-feed
■ early introduction of weaning foods
■ insisting baby 'eats everything up'
■ too many snacks
■ lack of opportunity and encouragement for physical activity – long periods of time spent in cot, pram, bouncing chair or playpen.

Prevention and management

The infant's weight and height measurements should be plotted on a percentile chart (growth chart, see page 132) to determine by how much she is above the ideal for her age. The aim is to slow down the rate of weight gain or temporarily halt it. A *slow* weight loss may be desirable in the older baby (9–12 months) if there is marked obesity, but remember that babies need a nutritious diet at all times.

Practical measures include:

■ encouraging mothers to breast-feed
■ making up bottle-feeds correctly – no added sugar or solids
■ avoidance of early weaning (not before 6 months) (see Weaning, Chapter 4, pages 70–7)
■ allowing the baby's appetite to dictate how much food is eaten – encourage finger foods and self-feeding

- providing opportunity and encouragement for physical activity in a safe environment
- liaison between nursery staff and parent/carer:
  - keep a record of food and drink intake
  - the amount of milk should not exceed 1 pint a day as solid food increases
  - avoid offering sugary foods and drinks
- regular growth checks – record the measurements on the baby's percentile chart (see page 132).

OVERWEIGHT AND OBESITY IN CHILDHOOD

The effects may include:
- appearance – the child looks fat (plump abdomen, thighs and upper arms; when standing straight the ankles, knees and thighs are touching). Knock-knees are common and there may be back and posture problems
- measurements of the skin folds around the upper arms, just below the waist and below the shoulder blades will be above normal
- above 'ideal' weight and height measurements – a child may be taller than expected due to increased protein intake
- difficulty with gross motor skills – PE, games and sports
- embarrassment at having to change for games and swimming
- being teased and called 'fatty', leading to poor self-image and possibly refusing to go to school
- social isolation
- difficulty in buying/choosing clothes – clothes often several sizes bigger than recommended age-size.

Possible causes are:
- a pattern of eating large meals
- snacking and grazing on high-calorie foods, often sitting down to do so
- lack of physical exercise
- economic and psychological factors.

Prevention and management
It is easier to guide children towards good eating habits when they are very young. As they get older they are more strongly influenced by their peer group and advertising. Sensible nutrition and daily exercise is the best prevention against overweight and can be undertaken by all family members.

Major changes to a child's eating pattern must be planned and supervised by the doctor or community dietician in consultation with the child and her parents. The aim is to prevent further weight gain, or achieve a *very gradual loss*, bearing in mind that the child is still growing physically and mentally and needs adequate nutrition to do so. Severe dieting and calorie restriction is inappropriate for young children. Consistent and regular support for the child and her family is important to bring about improvement. Nursery and school staff can play a vital part in offering such support.

A child's nutritional plan will be based around three appealing, nutritious meals a day, plus two or three healthy snacks. Foods and drinks should include:

- starchy carbohydrates (including wholegrains): bread, pasta, rice, also potatoes and other starchy vegetables
- reduced intake of sugary carbohydrate foods such as sweets, cakes and biscuits, chocolate and fizzy drinks
- proteins such as lean meat, fish, milk, cheese, eggs (or alternatives)
- fresh fruit and vegetables for vitamin, mineral and fibre content
- not more than 1 pint of milk a day – semi-skimmed is likely to be recommended if the child is over 2 years of age
- readily available drinks of fresh tap water
- occasional crisps and sweets
- vitamin supplements.

Encourage parents to:

- create healthy eating habits for all the family rather than singling out the child for dietary change
- place healthy snacks within the child's reach
- ensure plenty of opportunity for indoor and outdoor physical activity whatever the age of the child. Family members should also take part in exercise and activities with the child
- help their child towards independence in eating and drinking – this can prevent over-zealous feeding practices by parents or carers
- limit television and computer time for the whole family
- avoid constant discussion about weight
- reward progress with, for example, a special outing, a new item of clothing or book
- pressurise the government to ban television advertisements for junk food.

Growth measurements should be recorded at regular intervals.

REMEMBER!

For a healthier weight to be achieved, the parents and child must all understand the need for dietary change, and be informed, involved and co-operative throughout. Without resolve and co-operation the efforts will fail.

OVERWEIGHT AND OBESITY IN ADULTHOOD

Overweight children may become overweight adults with health risks of:
■ coronary heart disease
■ raised blood pressure
■ chest infections
■ varicose veins
■ arthritis
■ postural problems
■ possible infertility
■ greater risk of accidents and toxaemia of pregnancy
■ shorter life expectancy.

UNDERWEIGHT

If a child's appetite is generally poor over a period of time, or if a child is not gaining weight, a check-up from the doctor is necessary to try and establish the cause. Make meals and snacks appetising and appealing, offering small, regular meals of foods with a high calorie content (see also Faltering growth, page 130).

Iron-deficiency anaemia

Iron deficiency anaemia is the most usual form of anaemia in children. Lack of iron prevents the production of haemoglobin, a protein in red blood cells, which transports oxygen around the body.

Iron is stored in the foetal liver during the last weeks of pregnancy and a baby born at term has sufficient stored iron for the first 6 months of life. Although breast milk is very low in iron, it is well absorbed (see also Chapter 4, page 58), but from around 6 months a breast-fed baby needs other sources of dietary iron. Formula milks, including follow-on formulae, are fortified with iron.

Those most at risk of iron-deficiency anaemia are:
■ pre-term babies, because they lack stores of iron
■ infants who are given cow's milk instead of breast or formula milk before 12 months of age
■ toddlers, especially those in low **socio-economic** families
■ children of any age whose nutrition is inadequate. Older babies and toddlers with small appetites and a reluctance to eat solids are also at risk
■ children who eat a vegan diet
■ fussy eaters
■ children whose iron absorption ability is reduced, for example, in coeliac condition (see Chapter 7, pages 110–13).

RECOGNISING ANAEMIA IN CHILDREN

A child with anaemia is likely to look pale. The mucous membranes inside the eyelids and mouth will also be pale – possibly the only noticeable areas of pallor in a child with black skin. You may notice that the child tires quickly, lacks energy and is breathless during physical activity. Other signs can include poor appetite, irritability, frequent infections and delayed growth. Nausea, vomiting and fainting may occur. A low haemoglobin level in a blood test indicates anaemia.

TREATMENT AND PREVENTION OF ANAEMIA

Treatment
Iron-rich foods (see Chapter 2, Table 2.2, page 26), plus iron supplements in the form of medicine, or tablets for older children, are the mainstay of treatment and are bulleted here:

■ The best dietary iron is **haem iron**. It is found in red meat and offal (liver, kidney and heart) and is easily absorbed by the body. Young children may find red meat or liver more palatable if is finely chopped and cooked in casseroles and mince dishes. Red meat consumption has markedly fallen due to the BSE and vCJD crises (see Chapter 6, page 97).

■ **Non-haem iron**, present in plant and vegetable foods such as pulses, cereals, green leafy vegetables, dried fruit and cocoa, is less well absorbed so it is important that adequate vitamin C, which assists the absorption of iron, is provided with these foods. For example: a portion of Weetabix and a diluted pure orange drink; vegetarian curry, mixed bean and lentil lasagne or casserole and a piece of fresh fruit; cheese and onion quiche served with green salad and tomatoes. Offer breakfast cereals fortified with iron.

■ Iron medicine or tablets. Iron medicine is best taken through a straw as it tends to discolour the teeth. Always encourage teeth cleaning after medicine has been taken. Never put the medicine into food. Iron supplements will turn the stools black.

SAFE PRACTICE

■ Always give the correct prescribed dose of iron medicine or tablets. An overdose can cause stomach upsets or poisoning.
■ Make a written record of iron medicine or tablets given to a child in the nursery, school or childminder's home.

Prevention

Encourage regular and healthy meals and snacks by offering a variety of foods from the four main food groups (see The food groups, Chapter 2, pages 28–9). Discourage 'snacking' on high-calorie foods from the fifth food group, which leave little room for essential nutritious foods.

Activity

Find out about and write up the following information:

1 Which medicines, if any, are parents/carers allowed to bring into nursery or school for their children?
2 Where are medicines stored?
3 What is the procedure for giving medicines and what details are recorded?

Faltering growth

Growth is a major factor in determining a child's health. It is measured in terms of:

■ weight
■ height
■ head circumference.

MEASUREMENT OF GROWTH

Growth is measured and recorded on percentile charts. Different charts are used for boys and girls, and for babies under 1 year two charts may be used.

One is for babies who are born pre-term, allowing head circumference and weight measurements to be recorded and charted from 20 weeks' gestation up to the expected date of delivery (EDD).

The second chart is used with the majority of babies and plots the growth of babies born from 30 weeks' gestation and up to 52 weeks or 1 year. Measurements of head circumference, length and weight are taken, and can be charted on the graph at regular intervals during the first year.

HOW TO RECORD

The birth measurement is an important starting point from which all other recordings are compared. A single measurement of a baby, which has no other measurement to compare with, is meaningless. It cannot indicate a deviation or growth pattern.

Accurate recording of the gestational age of a baby (the number of weeks spent in utero) must be the starting point from which other measurements follow. Three measurements are generally taken in babies born at term: weight, length and head circumference.

Weight
The birth weight is taken and recorded following delivery. Subsequent weighing should be undertaken with the baby naked, using regularly balance, calibrated scales. This frequently takes place in the child health clinic by the health visitor.

Length
This may be difficult to record accurately in a small baby and two people are needed using a measuring mat with a head and a footboard. The baby must be supine with one person holding the baby's head against the headboard and the second bringing the footboard up to the heels. The knees should be gently pressed down to help ensure the legs are flat.

Head circumference
This is especially important in the first 6 months of life. A non-stretchable, thin metal or plastic tape is placed around the largest part of the head, midway between the eyebrows and the hairline at the front and the most prominent part of the skull at the back.

PATTERNS OF MEASUREMENTS

These three measurements are plotted on the percentile chart (see page 132). Growth should follow a steady path on the chart and each baby will have her own individual pattern. An average-sized baby will generally follow the 50th centile line, a very large baby possibly above the 98th centile and a very small baby the 9th centile or less. There are variations according to a baby's ethnic background; African-Caribbean babies, for example, may be slightly above the 50th centile, while Asian babies may be slightly below it.

Babies and young children who fail to gain adequate weight are said to have 'faltering growth' (previously known as failure to thrive). They neither gain weight nor grow as expected because:
- they are unable to take in and retain food, or
- there are feeding difficulties, or
- insufficient food is being offered.

Faltering growth is a common and complex condition in which medical, socioeconomic and emotional difficulties often overlap. It can occur in any family and across the whole social spectrum. Causes may include:
- poor sucking ability due to prematurity, cleft palate and/or lip or generally poor muscle tone

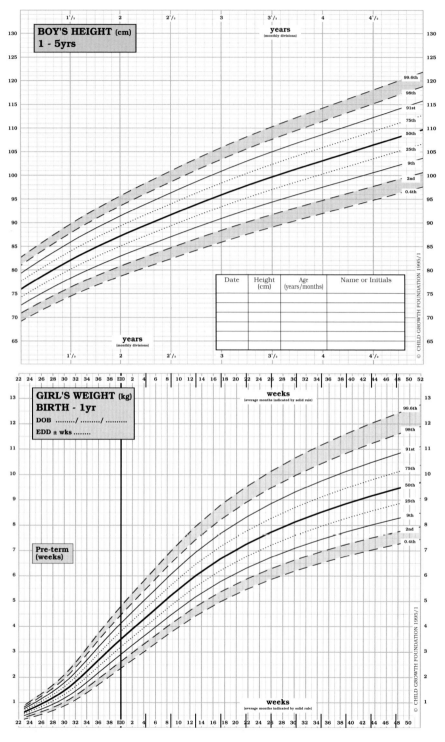

Examples of percentile charts

- kidney and intestinal disorders, congenital heart disease, severe asthma or any other condition that causes breathlessness and makes feeding difficult and tiring
- disorders of metabolism and poor nutrient absorption – for example, cystic fibrosis and phenylketonuria, also food allergies and intolerances such as coeliac condition
- special needs – for example, feeding, eating and drinking may be slow and difficult for children with cerebral palsy or Down syndrome
- difficulty in establishing a feeding pattern (whether breast or formula feeding), leaving the mother exhausted
- a stressful parent–child relationship in which a mother may lack confidence in caring for her child, or feels a failure in her mothering ability. She may be unaware of her child's needs and have difficulty in responding to them
- maternal ill health. A mother may have physical or emotional difficulties, or suffer from post-natal depression or other depressive illness. She may also lack support for her own needs
- a child's difficult behaviour pattern during mealtimes. Weaning may be a demanding time with the infant refusing solids. An older baby or toddler may be reluctant to eat or show distress and turn away when offered food, making mealtimes a source of tension and undermining parents' efforts to make sure the child has adequate nutrition
- inappropriate nutrition. Some children receive inappropriate diets because parents or carers apply the principles of a high fibre/low fat diet, recommended for adult health, when preparing their children's meals. This type of nutrition will not provide children with sufficient calories for growth and energy requirements, and essential minerals and vitamins may be missing or poorly absorbed
- insufficient or over-dilute formula feeds
- reliance on convenience foods because of lack of cooking facilities, for example, in hostel accommodation
- child abuse or neglect, leading to deprivation of food.

CARE AND SUPPORT FOR THE CHILD AND FAMILY

The initial aim of care and support for the child who has faltering growth is to find out the underlying problem and promote weight gain. An examination to exclude a medical cause is usually the starting point. There may be a clearly defined cause for faltering growth that can be treated. However, there is usually no one, single cause and a multidisciplinary approach, possibly with input from the family doctor, paediatrician or nutritionist, health visitor and Early Years worker, is the most appropriate way forward.

Early Years workers in a nursery or home setting need to be familiar with and fully involved in any care and support plan. The aim will be to help the child to feed successfully and take in adequate nutrition, so enabling her to reach the required weight. At the same time parents' needs (especially the mother's) must be recognised and supported. A mother whose child is not thriving will feel anxious. Listening to her concerns and allowing her to express her feelings in a calm, unhurried atmosphere will be an important part of professional care.

Extra visits from the health visitor and community nursery nurse can be effective. Practical help and advice with infant feeding and weaning can be offered, and helpful suggestions aimed at making mealtimes more relaxed and inviting for a child can be sensitively discussed – for example, offering small portions of food on small plates, giving praise when food is eaten, promoting a calm atmosphere. The less stressful mealtimes are, the more confident parents will become. Supervising the child's progress over a period of time and offering encouragement to the family is crucial for a successful outcome.

Referral to other support agencies (for example, social services), day care provision or short-term admission to hospital may be considered for some children.

REMEMBER!

Medical disorders on their own and child abuse or neglect account for only a small number of children with faltering growth.

The Children's Society's report, 'When Feeding Fails' (2000), offers an insight into the experiences and concerns of a number of parents who encountered feeding difficulties with their children.

Vitamin deficiency disorders

Vitamin deficiency disorders occur either from a lack of a particular vitamin in the diet or as a result of failure of absorption due to an intestinal problem. Breast milk contains all the vitamins a baby needs as long as the mother's diet is balanced and varied. Formula milks are fortified with vitamins.

Although vitamin deficiencies are relatively uncommon, the rapid growth and development taking place in infancy and childhood makes deficiency a possibility, and rickets and scurvy are still seen in children. Rickets, due to a lack of vitamin D, is more commonly seen among Asian children. There may be a combination of causes – genetic factors, traditional dress customs resulting in less exposure to sunlight, lack of vitamin

D in the typical Asian diet of cereals and vegetables, and over-processing of western foods.

Margarine, eggs, whole milk and oily fish (all sources of vitamin D) can be included in the diet. Daily vitamin A, D and C supplements from the onset of weaning up to 5 years will ensure adequate vitamin intake for all children, especially those who may be receiving poor diets or going through a fussy stage of eating. Vitamin drops should not be put in a baby's bottle – he may not finish his feed, and also some drops will stick to the side of the bottle.

The times of greatest risk of vitamin deficiency are:
- during weaning when feeding moves from a milk diet to solid foods
- during the toddler stage when food fads are common
- during illness
- in restricted diets, such as vegan, low-fat and macrobiotic diets, and in cases of food allergy or intolerance.

Infants need large amounts of calcium because of their fast growth rate and vitamin D is needed for calcium absorption. Because sunshine is the best source of vitamin D, they are particularly at risk of deficiency if kept indoors for long periods, covered up too much when outdoors or if sunshine is scarce.

Table 8.1 on the next page lists the main vitamin deficiency disorders and their treatment.

Dental caries

Dental caries (tooth decay) is an extremely common problem among young children. It leads to pain, fillings and extractions. It is not uncommon to see pre-school children with several filled teeth and gaps where teeth have been extracted. The diagram on page 138 shows the progress of tooth decay.

Sugary foods and drinks are the main cause of tooth decay. The longer sugars remain in the mouth, the greater the damage will be. Children who do not eat sweets and sugary foods or drink sweet drinks are less likely to need fillings and extractions. Tooth extractions in the years before natural loss of deciduous (milk) teeth can lead to gum shrinkage as well as eating, speech and emotional problems.

It is unrealistic to ban sweets and sugary foods altogether, but understanding the relationship between eating sugars and tooth decay helps adults to care for children's teeth correctly. Dental caries is preventable by appropriate nutrition (meals, snacks and drinks), regular teeth cleaning routines and dental inspections.

Table 8.1 Vitamin deficiency disorders

Vitamin	Disorder	Signs and symptoms of deficiency	Treatment	Notes
Vitamin A	1 Night blindness 2 Skin and respiratory problems 3 Xerophthalmia leading to blindness	1 Inability to see in dim light 2 ■ Dry, scaly, roughened skin ■ Itchy skin and eyes ■ Respiratory tract infections 3 Softening of cornea and eye infections causing permanent eye damage	■ Large doses vitamin A ■ Diet rich in dairy foods and fish liver oils ■ Dark green, yellow and orange vegetables and fruit	■ Vitamin supplements and fortified margarine make deficiency rare, although it still occurs in India and Africa, where many children become blind
Vitamin B$_1$	Beri-beri	■ Listlessness and irritability ■ Poor appetite ■ Vomiting and constipation ■ Nerve damage leading to pain in legs and feet ■ Heart enlargement The onset may be acute in infants, causing heart problems	■ Vitamin B$_1$ supplement ■ Diet rich in thiamin – pulses, egg yolk, liver, fortified cereals	■ Occurs mainly in countries where polished (white) rice is the staple food. Polishing/refining the rice removes the husk containing vitamin B$_1$
Folic acid/folate	1 Anaemia 2 Neural tube defects	1 See pages 128–30 2 Spina bifida and anencephaly (abnormalities of the spinal cord and brain) are linked to folic acid deficiency	1 Management of anaemia (see page 129) and folic acid supplements 2 Management and treatment according to baby's needs	■ Iron and folic acid supplements recommended before conception and in early pregnancy plus diet rich in wholegrains, meat, dark leafy vegetables, carrots, milk ■ Malabsorption of folic acid often occurs in coeliac disease

Table 8.1 Vitamin deficiency disorders *(continued)*

Vitamin	Disorder	Signs and symptoms of deficiency	Treatment	Notes
Niacin	Pellagra	■ Loss of weight ■ Rough, thickened skin with reddish/brown areas appearing on face, neck and hands ■ Irritability ■ Diarrhoea ■ Mental confusion	■ Niacin supplements ■ Bread and maize fortified with Niacin	■ Mostly seen in Africa and India where maize, a poor source of Niacin, is a staple food
Vitamin C	Scurvy	■ Swollen, bleeding gums ■ Tendency to bruise easily ■ Painful, tender limbs ■ Poor resistance to infection ■ Anaemia	■ Vitamin C supplements ■ Fresh citrus fruits ■ Fresh vegetables	■ Vitamin C easily lost in cooking and exposure to air ■ Pain is quickly relieved once treatment is started
Vitamin D	Rickets	■ Delayed closure of anterior fontanelle ■ Soft, deformed bones ■ Painful joints ■ Postural deformities – bow legs, curvature of spine ■ Poor muscle tone ■ Delayed motor development and dentition ■ 'Rickety rosary' – prominent beads of cartilage down sides of ribs	■ Large doses vitamin D ■ At least 1 pint milk daily for calcium content ■ No weight bearing until bones and joints are healing	■ Children who receive little exposure to sunlight may be at risk of deficiency ■ Diets in which cereals and vegetables are staple foods are likely to be deficient in vitamin D

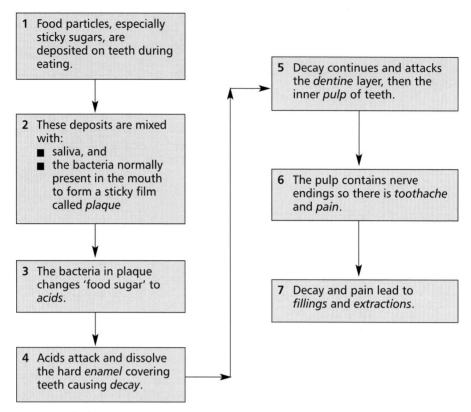

1 Food particles, especially sticky sugars, are deposited on teeth during eating.

2 These deposits are mixed with:
  ■ saliva, and
  ■ the bacteria normally present in the mouth to form a sticky film called *plaque*

3 The bacteria in plaque changes 'food sugar' to *acids*.

4 Acids attack and dissolve the hard *enamel* covering teeth causing *decay*.

5 Decay continues and attacks the *dentine* layer, then the inner *pulp* of teeth.

6 The pulp contains nerve endings so there is *toothache* and *pain*.

7 Decay and pain lead to *fillings* and *extractions*.

How tooth decay occurs

Carers can promote dental health in children by following these guidelines:

■ Do not offer babies and young children dummies dipped in sugar or honey, or bottles of sugar water or sugary fruit drinks. Check labels on herbal and fruit drinks – they may say 'no added sweetening', but may be high in natural sugar and should be well diluted before giving them to a baby or young child. Cooled, boiled water should be offered in preference to fruit drinks. Weaning foods should be as sugar-free as possible. Foods that encourage a baby to chew can be offered from around 7 months.

■ Offer children a well-balanced diet. Include raw fruit and vegetables (apples, carrots, celery) and wholegrain foods, all of which encourage chewing. Chewing increases the blood supply to the teeth, gums and jaws, aiding their healthy growth and development and helping normal speech. It also increases the flow of saliva, which helps to keep the teeth clean.

■ Discourage sweets, biscuits, sticky, chewy foods and fizzy drinks etc., especially if they are going to be eaten or drunk over a period of time.

Sweets, if given, are best offered at a specific time (perhaps after a meal), followed by thorough teeth cleaning.

REMEMBER!

Eating and drinking sugary food and drinks automatically increases acid production in the mouth.
■ Start dental care as soon as the first tooth appears. Wipe over the tooth and gums with a clean, non-fluffy cloth or use a small toothbrush and a tiny amount of toothpaste. Young children should clean their teeth in the morning and last thing at night, as well as after meals and after eating sweets. In many nurseries, children have the opportunity to clean their teeth after meals.

REMEMBER!

Cleaning teeth is a difficult task to perform correctly, especially the inner aspect of the back teeth, and young children need help and supervision.
■ The mineral fluoride guards against tooth decay by protecting the enamel from acid attack. It is found naturally in the drinking water in some areas, while in others it has been added. Where there is no fluoridation of water, fluoride drops or tablets may be prescribed. Too much fluoride can cause softening of the teeth as well as brown staining, white mottling and delayed shedding. Many toothpastes now contain fluoride but only small amounts should be used.
■ Regular dental check-ups, starting in the second year, are recommended. The dentist will advise on fluoride treatment and the correct technique for cleaning teeth.

Teething is often wrongly blamed for a range of symptoms and infections, which many babies and toddlers are likely to experience during their first two to three years, for example, a raised temperature, coughs and colds, ear infections, diarrhoea and nappy rash. Never be tempted to think 'it's just teething troubles'. A baby or toddler who is unwell must be seen by the family doctor.

Activity
1 Ask the children in your placement how often they eat sweets – every day? once a week? never?
2 Ask them how frequently they clean their teeth and, if they are able to tell you, when they last visited the dentist.
3 Collate your information and set it out as a pie chart or histogram. Ask your college tutor for help with this.

Constipation

Constipation is the passing of hard, infrequent and possibly painful stools. The longer the amount of time faeces remain in the lower bowel the greater the risk of constipation. It is a common problem in young children and causes distress for them and their parents. A situation may develop in which a child is frightened to pass a stool and the longer she delays the greater the discomfort and difficulty. Sometimes straining to pass a hard stool causes an anal fissure – a small crack in the mucous membrane of the anus – with some spotting of blood. This causes further pain.

Possible causes of constipation include:
■ poor diet with insufficient fibre and fluid intake
■ toddlers drinking too much milk and eating insufficient solid food
■ illness or operation, leading to reduction in a child's food intake
■ early toilet training
■ mismanagement of toilet training, with too little time for toileting routine and over-emphasis on bowel function
■ emotional problems leading to 'stool holding'.

PREVENTION OF CONSTIPATION

Make sure children's diets contain fibre in the form of wholegrain foods, fresh fruit and vegetables. Fibre keeps the faeces bulky, because it is not digested, and soft, because it absorbs water in the large intestine. Bulky, soft faeces are easy to pass. Offer extra drinks of water during the day. Diluted fresh orange juice or prune juice may be helpful. Laxatives should only be given with medical approval. Emotional causes of constipation may be more difficult to resolve and require specialist help. Management of toilet training is covered widely in other textbooks.

Nutrition for an unwell child

From time to time Early Years workers will care for a child who is unwell, whether for a few hours in the setting until he is collected by his carer or, if working as a nanny, for longer periods in the home. Common reasons for a child feeling unwell are:
■ upper respiratory infections – colds, sore throats, sinusitis, tonsillitis, croup
■ ear infections
■ infectious diseases such as meales, mumps, whooping cough, rubella, chickenpox

■ diarrhoea and vomiting (see below).

Children who are unwell, especially if they have diarrhoea and vomiting, can quickly become dehydrated. Signs of dehydration in a young child include: thirst and dry parched mouth; sunken eyes; depressed anterior fontanelle in infants; scanty urine output or dry nappies in infants; quickened, weak pulse and low blood pressure.

Nutrition for an unwell child depends very much on how he feels, his appetite, his ability to chew and swallow and any medical instructions from the doctor. A child with a raised temperature who is fighting infection may only take sips or drinks of clear fluids during the first 24 hours. This is quite normal. Fluid intake is important to bring down a temperature and prevent dehydration. Do not try to make the child eat if he is not interested in solid food. Be flexible when reintroducing solids, as illness is a time when some of the rules regarding Group Five ('occasional') foods can be broken.

General guidelines for offering food and drink to an unwell child include:

■ encourage fluid intake – in addition to plain water, offer lemon barley water, lemonade or whatever fizzy drinks a child enjoys, as they are quickly absorbed and the sugar content provides energy. Water for infants under 1 year must be boiled and cooled
■ offer light, nutritious food – a little and often. Small portions of soup, egg custard, milk puddings, favourite yoghurts, jelly and ice-cream and slices of fruit may tempt a child. Small, thin, crustless sandwiches with favourite fillings, or 'soldiers' of bread and butter can be appetising
■ encourage milk foods – milk is very nutritious and can be given in a variety of ways, for example yoghurt, fromage frais, milk shakes, warm chocolate drink, or custard. (For milk in diarrhoea and vomiting, see page 142.)

A child with mumps or a sore throat may find it easier to eat puréed or semi-solid foods. Provide interesting drinking straws or a 'special' beaker to encourage him to drink plenty of fluids. Older children may enjoy sucking a home-made ice lolly.

REMEMBER!

■ A child with whooping cough frequently vomits so nutritious fluids are very important. Special high calorie drinks may be advised by the doctor.
■ Encourage fluid intake for any child who is unwell.

DIARRHOEA AND VOMITING

Diarrhoea (frequent, loose, watery stools) and vomiting can occur separately or together. For diarrhoea to occur, something (often infection) causes quickened peristalsis and the rapid movement of food and drink through the intestines before absorption of nutrients and water can take place.

The cause of vomiting may not always be immediately obvious but must never be ignored.

Management of diarrhoea and vomiting

The aim is to prevent dehydration. Seek medical advice urgently for a baby or young child with a combination of diarrhoea and vomiting, or if she appears unwell with either diarrhoea or vomiting. She may need to be admitted to hospital for intravenous fluid therapy.

If a baby has diarrhoea but is not vomiting:

■ breast-feeding can continue but stop formula feeds (they can make the diarrhoea worse) and offer the baby drinks of cooled, boiled water or well-diluted fruit juice
■ stop all solid foods, whether the baby is breastfed or formula fed
■ oral rehydration solution (glucose, sodium and potassium), such as Dioralyte or Rehydrat may be prescribed by the doctor. It must be carefully made up and given according to the instructions
■ formula feeds and solid food can be introduced after 24 hours if the baby responds to the rehydration fluids and the diarrhoea settles.

'Toddler diarrhoea' is a recognised condition in which diarrhoea occurs for several days at a time. The stools contain undigested food. The child appears well and active, and there is usually no cause for concern although a check-up with the doctor is advisable. As the toddler gets older the diarrhoea ceases.

For older children

It may be all right to wait 24 hours to see if there is any improvement in a child's diarrhoea or vomiting before calling the doctor, unless he is obviously unwell. The same principles of stopping milk and solids and offering rehydration and other clear fluids apply. Milk and solids can be reintroduced gradually after 24 hours if the diarrhoea and vomiting has stopped, so that a child is eating a normal diet within three to four days.

SPECIAL FEEDING METHODS

For medical reasons some children receive their nutrition (special paediatric feeds) through a tube, which may either pass via the nose into the stomach or be inserted directly into the stomach or small intestine. This is called **enteral nutrition** and is necessary for maintaining normal growth when a child is unable to take in adequate nutrition orally. For example, a baby or child may have difficulty in sucking or swallowing effectively, or may have a serious heart, kidney or liver condition. Enteral nutrition may be temporary or permanent, but can only be carried out if the gastrointestinal tract is working well and able to absorb the nutrients. You may care for a child in a day care or education setting, or in the home, who receives long-term or short-term enteral nutrition. The community or hospital paediatric nurse will provide training and advice to manage this method of feeding. Never attempt this procedure without prior training and without permission from the child's parents or carer.

If the gastrointestinal tract is no longer functioning properly **parenteral nutrition** will be necessary, that is, feeding nutritious fluids directly into a large vein in the child's body. It is a more highly skilled and complicated procedure than enteral feeding. It can be managed in the home but only if parents and carers are offered careful training and 24-hour specialist back-up support and advice. Parents already anxious and worried by their child's condition, may find the procedure too emotionally and physically exhausting to supervise at home and prefer their child to remain in hospital.

QUICK CHECK

1 What are the possible causes of overweight/obesity in infancy?
2 How might obesity affect:
   (a) a baby's physical development?
   (b) an older child's emotional development?
3 What practical measures could you take to prevent overweight/obesity in infants?
4 What might lead to think that a child in your care is anaemic?
5 Name the best sources of haem-iron.
6 If a child in your care eats a vegetarian diet how could you ensure her intake of dietary iron was being effectively absorbed?
7 What do you understand by the term 'faltering growth'?
8 What are the main 'care and support' aims for a child with faltering growth and his family?
9 What is the role of the Early Years worker when caring for a child with faltering growth?
10 (a) Name the vitamin that is lacking in the conditions of rickets and scurvy
   (b) What are the main sources of vitamins C and D?
11 What might be the effects of dental extractions on a pre-school child?
12 (a) How does the mineral fluoride guard against tooth decay?
   (b) What are the dangers to teeth of too much fluoride?
13 What sensible dietary principles would you follow to prevent, as far as possible, constipation in children?

14 **(a)** Name four common conditions that lead to a child feeling unwell.
(b) Give two reasons why fluids are important for a child who is
unwell.

15 What do you understand by 'enteral' and 'parenteral' feeding?

KEY WORDS AND TERMS

*You need to know what these words and phrases mean. Go back through
the chapter and find out.*

dehydration	oral rehydration
enteral feeding	overweight
faltering growth	parenteral feeding
fluoride	percentile chart
haem iron	plaque
haemoglobin	rickets
non-haem iron	scurvy
obesity	

SAFE FOOD PREPARATION

This chapter covers:
- basic food hygiene
- food storage and processing
- food labelling and additives

Basic food hygiene

When preparing and handling food for children, it is essential to maintain the highest standards of hygiene to prevent the spread of infections. Such infections are caused by harmful micro-organisms, known as **pathogens**, which contaminate (or spoil) the food when hygiene standards are not maintained.

CAUSES OF FOOD CONTAMINATION

The main causes of food contamination are bacteria, viruses, **moulds** and **yeasts**.

Bacteria
Bacteria are small, living organisms that are around us all the time. Most are harmless and some are even beneficial – those that live in our guts to digest foods, for example. However, some types of bacteria can affect flavours, cause food to smell and even cause food poisoning.

Viruses
Viruses are tiny – smaller than bacteria. They only grow on living tissue and so cannot live in food. They are less significant in contamination of food than bacteria, but can cause food-related illness, such as hepatitis A, an infection of the liver causing jaundice and, less commonly, food poisoning.

Moulds
Moulds are tiny plants, which form complex networks that we cannot see. They need oxygen to grow and because of this are usually seen only on the surface of foods. They can produce toxic substances that can penetrate foods.

Yeasts

Yeasts occur naturally on the surface of fruits and are also present in the air and soil. They multiply by 'budding' – producing buds that break off. Yeasts ferment sugars present in food to produce carbon dioxide and alcohol. This can be helpful, for example in the production of wines, but it can also cause spoilage of jams, etc.

Some contamination may be caused during food production. The use of chemicals, insecticides etc. can affect our foods. As with viruses, these are much less likely to cause food poisoning than bacteria.

CONDITIONS FOR FOOD CONTAMINATION

For pathogens to thrive they need food, warmth, moisture and time.

Food

Bacteria, the most likely source of food poisoning, prefer certain foods to others. Cooked meats and meat products, gravies and stocks, milk, eggs and products made from them, shellfish and cooked rice all attract and encourage the growth of bacteria.

Some foods, however, have additives that inhibit bacterial growth. These include sugars, salt, preservatives and acids. Vacuum packaging, where oxygen has been removed, can also prevent deterioration. All of these limit bacteria multiplication to some extent.

Warmth

Blood heat is an ideal temperature for bacteria to grow. So temperatures higher than 63°C and lower than 5°C are fairly safe.

Most bacteria are killed by a constant temperature of at least 70°C that reaches to all parts of the food. At temperatures of below 5°C (the correct temperature for refrigeration), bacteria do not grow and a few will die, but when food is returned to warm conditions multiplication will begin again.

SAFE PRACTICE

'Cool' spots from food reheated in a microwave can allow bacteria to breed. Reheated food must always be stirred and piping hot.

Moisture

Many of the high-risk foods contain moisture, which is essential for bacterial growth.

REMEMBER!

- Bacteria will multiply when fluids are added to reconstituted dried foods.
- The water in frozen foods (which is ice) is not available to the bacteria and provides safe storage, but only while the food is fully frozen.

Time

Bacteria grow by multiplication. In an ideal temperature they will grow by many thousands every four to five hours.

Wipe and clear up crumbs and spills as you go.

CROSS-CONTAMINATION

It is important to remember that poor personal hygiene and poor kitchen hygiene practices will add pathogens to, or contaminate, healthy food (see the charts on pages 148–9). Effective hand washing is probably the most important infection control measure where food is prepared, stored or eaten. Teach children how to wash their hands properly, using soap and water, and cleaning the backs and fronts of hands, and in between their fingers. Always rinse thoroughly and dry with a clean towel, preferably a disposable one. The children will follow your example, so always wash your hands before handling any food. Younger children need to be supervised in hand washing but older children need to be reminded to include it as part of their routine before meals, snack and after using the lavatory.

Food storage and processing

HOW CAN WE GET THE BEST VALUE FROM OUR FOOD?

The nutritional content of any food will depend on:
- the composition of the raw food or ingredients as grown or bought
- the nutrients lost during storage, preparation or cooking and the addition of extra nutrients during manufacture
- how much is eaten
- the specific nutritional needs of the individual and whether these have already been met from other foods in the diet.

BUYING FOOD

Always buy from clean shops where assistants do not touch raw food with their bare hands, especially those foods that will not need to be cooked, such as cakes and cooked meats.

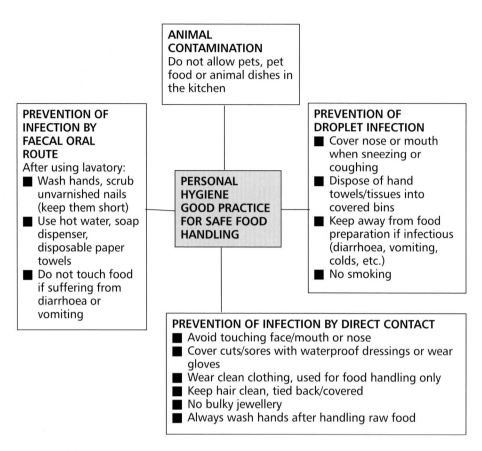

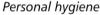

ANIMAL CONTAMINATION
Do not allow pets, pet food or animal dishes in the kitchen
PREVENTION OF INFECTION BY FAECAL ORAL ROUTE
After using lavatory:
■ Wash hands, scrub unvarnished nails (keep them short)
■ Use hot water, soap dispenser, disposable paper towels
■ Do not touch food if suffering from diarrhoea or vomiting
PERSONAL HYGIENE GOOD PRACTICE FOR SAFE FOOD HANDLING
PREVENTION OF DROPLET INFECTION
■ Cover nose or mouth when sneezing or coughing
■ Dispose of hand towels/tissues into covered bins
■ Keep away from food preparation if infectious (diarrhoea, vomiting, colds, etc.)
■ No smoking
PREVENTION OF INFECTION BY DIRECT CONTACT
■ Avoid touching face/mouth or nose
■ Cover cuts/sores with waterproof dressings or wear gloves
■ Wear clean clothing, used for food handling only
■ Keep hair clean, tied back/covered
■ No bulky jewellery
■ Always wash hands after handling raw food

Personal hygiene

REMEMBER!

- Check that the shop is cool and that perishables are kept in a refrigerated display cabinet.
- Check that cooked and uncooked foods are kept separate.
- Check that foods are within their sell-by or best before dates.

COOKING AND PRESERVATION

Most foods have to be prepared and cooked before they can be eaten. At each stage some of the nutrients will be lost or reduced. Further nutrients may be lost if the food is stored for long periods in conditions that are not ideal.

The aim is to keep these losses to a minimum, and fresh foods should be eaten wherever possible.

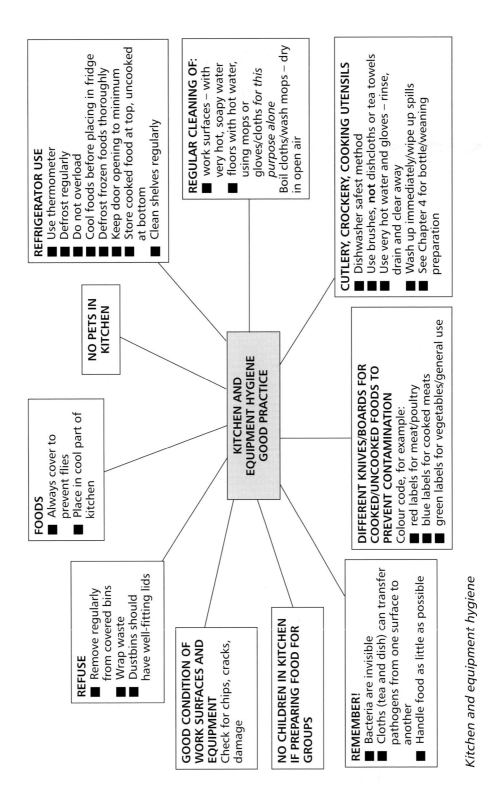

REFRIGERATOR USE
- Use thermometer
- Defrost regularly
- Do not overload
- Cool foods before placing in fridge
- Defrost frozen foods thoroughly
- Keep door opening to minimum
- Store cooked food at top, uncooked at bottom
- Clean shelves regularly

REGULAR CLEANING OF:
- work surfaces – with very hot, soapy water
- floors with hot water, using mops or gloves/cloths *for this purpose alone*
  Boil cloths/wash mops – dry in open air

CUTLERY, CROCKERY, COOKING UTENSILS
- Dishwasher safest method
- Use brushes, **not** dishcloths or tea towels
- Use very hot water and gloves – rinse, drain and clear away
- Wash up immediately/wipe up spills
- See Chapter 4 for bottle/weaning preparation

NO PETS IN KITCHEN

KITCHEN AND EQUIPMENT HYGIENE GOOD PRACTICE

FOODS
- Always cover to prevent flies
- Place in cool part of kitchen

DIFFERENT KNIVES/BOARDS FOR COOKED/UNCOOKED FOODS TO PREVENT CONTAMINATION
Colour code, for example:
- red labels for meat/poultry
- blue labels for cooked meats
- green labels for vegetables/general use

REFUSE
- Remove regularly from covered bins
- Wrap waste
- Dustbins should have well-fitting lids

GOOD CONDITION OF WORK SURFACES AND EQUIPMENT
Check for chips, cracks, damage

NO CHILDREN IN KITCHEN IF PREPARING FOOD FOR GROUPS

REMEMBER!
- Bacteria are invisible
- Cloths (tea and dish) can transfer pathogens from one surface to another
- Handle food as little as possible

Kitchen and equipment hygiene

Buying bread

Home cooking
Heat is generally applied to food in one of three ways:
■ directly, with or without additional fat – roasting, grilling, baking and microwave cooking
■ with water – boiling, stewing and braising
■ with fat – frying.
Heat causes chemical and physical changes in food, which in general improve flavour, palatability and digestibility. Heat may also increase the availability of some nutrients by destroying enzymes and anti-digestive factors. However, cooking more usually results in the loss of nutrients.

Aim to grill rather than fry foods. Grilling allows fat from foods to pass into the grill pan rather than being retained within the food.

Microwave cooking is quick with little nutrient loss. However, care needs to be taken to ensure previously cooked food is thoroughly reheated and piping hot.

Chopping foods such as fruit and vegetables a long time before cooking causes considerable vitamin loss. Try to prepare such foods just before cooking and plunge them into already boiling water. This will help reduce the loss of vitamins B and C.

REMEMBER!

The greatest nutrient losses are with:
■ high temperatures
■ long cooking times
■ large amounts of liquid.

PRESERVATION METHODS

Home freezing

Home freezing may result in some loss of Thiamin and vitamin C when vegetables are blanched in water before freezing, but less than would otherwise happen in storage. If the temperature of the freezer is kept below 218°C, there is almost no further loss of nutritional value until the food is thawed. In general, differences between the nutrient content of cooked fresh foods and cooked frozen foods are small.

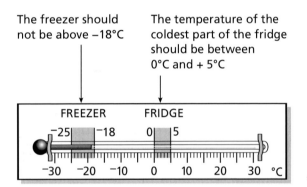

Temperatures for home storage in the fridge or freezer

Industrial processing

As with home freezing, the process itself has little effect on nutritional value and since the delay between harvesting and processing is minimal, the nutrients in the high quality fresh foods that are used are generally well retained.

Canning and bottling

The heat used in this process will reduce the amounts of heat-sensitive vitamins, especially Thiamin, folic acid and vitamin C. The losses will depend on the length of time needed to destroy pathogens and to cook the food. They will be greater for larger cans and in foods of close consistency, such as ham, because of the slow transfer of heat from the outside to the centre.

Dehydration
In carefully controlled conditions this has little effect on most nutrients, but about half the vitamin C is lost. Suitable packaging is important to limit further loss during long storage.

Irradiation
In the process of **irradiation**, food is exposed under controlled conditions to gamma rays from a radioactive source. But the food is not left radioactive.

The process is used to slow down the ripening process of fruits and vegetables, extend the shelf life of many foods, reducing storage problems, and to sterilise some products, such as chicken. It cannot be used on dairy products and oily fish because it alters their taste. It is thought that small losses of vitamin C, Thiamin, vitamin E and some fatty acids can occur, but the amounts are variable and dependent upon the dosages of gamma rays used.

ADDITIONAL SAFEGUARDS

With recent food scares and greater public awareness and interest in how our food is produced, the Food Standards Agency has been formed to oversee all aspects of food policy. Its essential aim is the protection of public health in relation to food. It is to develop a strategic view of food safety and standards from 'farm to fork'.

The agency has responsibility for many areas associated with food, including:
- investigating food safety and standards
- investigating food hygiene regulations and rules, food hazards and outbreaks of food-borne disease
- providing nutritional information
- enforcing food standards, promoting consumer choice, establishing clear and accurate food labelling
- setting standards and providing support for local authorities to enforce and monitor food law
- monitoring all aspects of meat hygiene; and developing policy on red meat, poultry and game. Developing strategies for control of BSE
- liaising with national and international bodies on all food issues
- developing effective communication with the public over all food issues
- drafting necessary legislation.

Low-fat Yoghurt
Pineapple

NUTRITION		
TYPICAL COMPOSITION	Each Pot (150g) provides	100g (3¹/₂oz) provide
Energy	608kJ/145kcal	405kJ/97kcal
Protein	8.6g	5.7g
Carbohydrate	25.8g	17.2g
of which sugars	25.8g	17.2g
Fat	1.4g	0.9g
of which saturates	0.8g	0.5g
polyunsaturates	0.2g	0.1g
Sodium	0.1g	0.1g
VITAMINS/ MINERALS	%RECOMMENDED DAILY AMOUNT	
Calcium	61	

INFORMATION

ADDED INGREDIENTS: SUGAR, PINEAPPLE, PINEAPPLE PUREE, STABILISERS (PECTIN, CAROB GUM), FLAVOURINGS

150 g e

DISPLAY UNTIL	USE BY
06OCT	08OCT
KEEP REFRIGERATED DO NOT FREEZE	

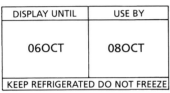

SUITABLE FOR
VEGETARIANS

Nutritional information

Activity

The label above tells you:

■ the name and description of the food
■ ingredients and energy content
■ composition, per pot and per 100 g
■ display/use by date and storage instructions
■ suitability of special dietary requirements.

What else might you need to know?

The main points to look for on food labels are:

■ the name or description of the food – by law this has to be clear and informative. A trade mark or brand name is not allowed as a substitute for a clear name and description of the food
■ where the food is made
■ how long and under what conditions the food can be kept – the 'best before' and 'use by' information. This is not necessary for all foods, for example sugar and sugar-based foods, fresh fruit and vegetables are exempt from this requirement. The label will also give

any instructions as to correct storage, for example in a cool dark
cupboard or in a refrigerator
■ weight, volume or number in the pack
■ place of origin
■ preparation or cooking instructions
■ name and address of the manufacturer.

Food labelling and additives

Food labels should tell us about the contents of a tin or packet, but they
can be very confusing.

If a manufacturer has voluntarily added vitamins or minerals to their
product or if they have made a nutritional claim (such as 'low fat' or 'main-
tains flexible joints'), they must give nutritional information on the packaging. Some manufacturers routinely provide nutritional information on
their products, even when not legally obliged to do so. Although there are
a few exceptions, most pre-packed foods are required to include a complete list of ingredients.

Although the actual quantities are not normally given, the ingredients
must be listed in descending order of weight – the first ingredient in the
list will be the one that weighed the most when it went into the food. The
presence of water, unless only a tiny amount, must also be indicated.

It is illegal for manufacturers to include false or misleading information
on their labels. However, many of the health and nutrition claims that
manufacturers make have yet to be defined in law. For example, the claim
'low fat' has already been defined – it refers to products that contain less
than 3 g fat per 100 g. The term 'helps maintain a healthy heart' has not
currently been defined. The Food Standards Agency is in the process of
drawing up rules to ensure that only claims defined by law can be used on
labels.

Some foods are genetically modified (GM). GM means advanced biological techniques are used to introduce new genetic characteristics into
plants and animals. They have been developed to give resistance to insect
pests and increase crop yields, benefiting world famine. However, worries
have been expressed over their possible effects on human health and
wildlife. Some experts fear that transplanted genes might cause allergic
reactions and increase resistance to antibiotics. New rules about the
labelling of GM foods were introduced in 2004. The Food Standards
Agency tells us that, 'In the EU, if a food contains or consists of genetically
modified organisms (GMOs), or contains ingredients produced from
GMOs, this must be indicated on the label. For GM products sold "loose",

information must be displayed immediately next to the food to indicate that it is GM Products produced with GM technology [cheese produced with GM enzymes, for example] do not have to be labelled. Products such as meat, milk and eggs from animals fed on GM animal feed also do not need to be labelled.' There is, however, pressure for GM-free labelling and a requirement to label if animals have been fed GM products.

TRAFFIC LIGHT LABELS

The Food Standards Agency advises cutting down on fat (particularly saturated fat), salt and added sugars. The agency has introduced Traffic Light labels to help consumers to see whether the foods they are considering buying contain high (red), medium (amber) or low (green) amounts of fat, saturated fat, sugars and salt. Here is what the Food Standards Agency has to say about the system:

- If you see a *red light*, you know the food is high in something we should be trying to cut down on. It's fine to have the food occasionally, or as a treat, but try to keep an eye on how often you choose these foods, or try eating them in smaller amounts.
- If you see an *amber light*, you know the food isn't high or low in the nutrient, so this is an OK choice most of the time, but you might want to go for green for that nutrient some of the time.
- If you see a *green light*, this means the food is low in that nutrient. The more green lights, the healthier the choice.

Many of the foods with traffic light colours that you see in the shops will have a mixture of red, amber and greens. So, when you're choosing between similar products, try to go for more greens and ambers, and fewer reds, if you want to make the healthier choice.

The amount in grams of each nutrient per serving is also given. This helps shoppers to compare products more easily. For instance, you can compare a similar product by two different manufacturers and choose the healthiest. For more information, visit www.eatwell.gov.uk/foodlabels/trafficlights.

The diagram on page 156 shows some examples of the traffic lights.

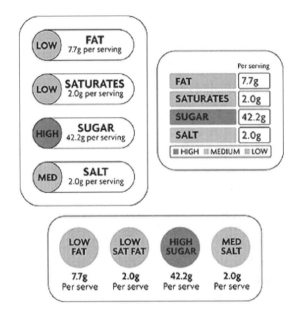

The Food Standards Agency's Traffic Light labels

ADDITIVES

A list of ingredients must also show any additives that have been used in the food. Most approved additives have an indentifying number – a simple coding system introduced to avoid long chemical names on labels. If the additive has been approved by the European Union as well as by the United Kingdom, there is an 'E' in front of the number. Usually a category name such as 'preservative' must come before the additive number to tell you why it has been included, for example 'Preservative E200'.

Flavourings that are used in very small amounts are not currently controlled in this way, although, like other additives, they can only be used in food if they are safe. Labels must state that flavourings have been used but need not list them.

Why are additives included?

Additives have several functions – as preservatives, colourings, flavour enhancers, emulsifiers and antioxidants (see below). They may be natural (sugar, salt, garlic, herbs) or artificial. Artificial additives may be modified natural substances or manufactured. They are identified by E numbers on food labels. Some children may develop allergies to an additive (see Hyperactivity, Chapter 6, page 105).

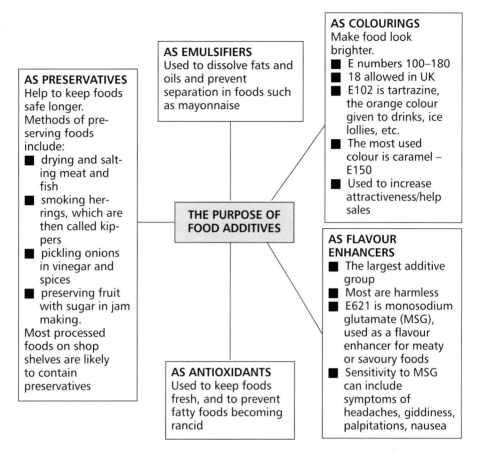

AS PRESERVATIVES
Help to keep foods safe longer.
Methods of preserving foods include:
- drying and salting meat and fish
- smoking herrings, which are then called kippers
- pickling onions in vinegar and spices
- preserving fruit with sugar in jam making.
Most processed foods on shop shelves are likely to contain preservatives

AS EMULSIFIERS
Used to dissolve fats and oils and prevent separation in foods such as mayonnaise

AS COLOURINGS
Make food look brighter.
- E numbers 100–180
- 18 allowed in UK
- E102 is tartrazine, the orange colour given to drinks, ice lollies, etc.
- The most used colour is caramel – E150
- Used to increase attractiveness/help sales

THE PURPOSE OF FOOD ADDITIVES

AS FLAVOUR ENHANCERS
- The largest additive group
- Most are harmless
- E621 is monosodium glutamate (MSG), used as a flavour enhancer for meaty or savoury foods
- Sensitivity to MSG can include symptoms of headaches, giddiness, palpitations, nausea

AS ANTIOXIDANTS
Used to keep foods fresh, and to prevent fatty foods becoming rancid

The purpose of food additives

Activity
Visit a local supermarket and look at the food labels on branded goods.
1   Is the information easily understood? Would it help you in meal planning?
2   Is there additional nutritional information provided by the supermarket? Would this be useful for you?
3   Do you consider that particular foods are given 'healthy' claims by this information? Do you consider this justified?

QUICK CHECK

1   What are bacteria and what effect can they have on food?
2   Describe the ideal conditions for pathogens to multiply when handling or preparing food.
3   How can yeasts affect foods?
4   List the foods that are most likely to be the source of food poisoning.
5   What is the safe temperature for a refrigerator?
6   Describe how you use a refrigerator to maintain a correct temperature.
7   Explain the term 'cross-contamination'.
8   List the personal hygiene measures essential for safe food handling.
9   What is the safest and most effective way of washing up?
10   Why does roast chicken contain more calories than grilled chicken?
11   Which preservation methods best retain water-soluble vitamins?
12   How can you tell if a food additive has been approved by the European Union?
13   What are the main reasons for including the following in food:
    (a) preservatives?
    (b) additives?
14   What is the difference between:
    (a) an emulsifier, and
    (b) an antioxidant?
15   Which is the most effective method of preserving water-soluble vitamins, bottling or freezing?

KEY WORDS AND TERMS

You need to know what these words and phrases mean. Go back through the chapter and find out.

Additives	Moulds
Dehydration	Pathogens
E numbers	Preservatives
Industrial processing	Toxins
Irradiation	Yeasts

10 PARTICULAR DIETARY PRACTICES

> **This chapter covers:**
> ■ **Multicultural diets**
> ■ **Vegetarian, vegan and other diets**

Multicultural diets

Increasingly, children are enjoying a wide variety of foods and ingredients from different cultural backgrounds. What were once 'exotic' foods, such as avocado, mango, pineapple, pizza, spaghetti and kebabs, are now readily available in supermarkets and family kitchens. Indeed, curry has overtaken fish and chips as the most popular food in Britain. So even children who are attending schools or nurseries in more remote areas in the UK now have access to interesting diets.

THE ADVANTAGES OF A MULTICULTURAL APPROACH TO DIET

These include the following:
■ children develop an awareness of and interest in other cultures
■ multi-ethnic foods often use less processed ingredients in their recipes and, as a result, are more natural
■ fruits alone are commonly used for desserts in many countries and there is less reliance on saturated fats, salty and sugary foods
■ offering foods from different cultures on school and nursery menus can promote self-respect in children from a variety of ethnic backgrounds, showing them that their culture is valued
■ children new to eating away from home will feel more secure when a familiar link – food – is provided
■ different tastes, textures and flavours enhance everyone's enjoyment and experience of food.

Childcare workers have a professional responsibility to support parents/carers in their decisions over special eating practices for their children, whether this is for religious, moral or health reasons.

Multi-ethnic foods often use less processed ingredients in their recipes

RELIGIOUS ASPECTS OF FOODS

Some dietary restrictions are closely linked to religion (see Table 10.1, pages 162–3), but how closely these are followed will vary from one religious (or cultural) group to another. Some groups will ignore them completely and others will adhere totally. It is important to find out family policy and not to make assumptions.

REMEMBER!

■ Many cultural groups will have periods of fasting, although children are usually exempt. Often a family meal will have been eaten at night, for example during Ramadan, and children may be tired the following day.
■ Always check with parents/carers about the special religious and cultural needs of any individual child.

CHANGES IN CULTURAL DIETS

Many diets of families from ethnic minority groups are now a combination of traditional and British foods. School-age children eat with and are influenced by their friends. British convenience foods are frequently advertised, easily available and cheap.

Local shops selling Indian, Caribbean or Jewish foods, for example, generally offer limited choices and may be more expensive. Families may have to travel further afield to obtain their own cultural foods, and this becomes especially difficult where there are only small groups of people wanting very special ethnic ingredients in their diets.

Children eating the Asian way – traditionally only the right hand is used to scoop up the food

Activity
1 Visit your nearest shop selling ethnic foods. Consider the variety of foods offered, including staples such as flours and rices.
   (a) Are the foods offered especially 'healthy', for example wholegrain, brown rices, less processing in flours, etc?
   (b) What would be the nutritional benefits of promoting these foods in a nursery?
   (c) Look at the fruit and vegetables on display. Are there foods that are new to you? Research their particular nutritional values.
   (d) Create a nursery menu for one week using dietary principles from a chosen ethnic group (see Table 10.1).
2 Many cultures have different ways of eating.
   (a) Research the 'tools' used at mealtimes and the ages at which children are encouraged to use them.
   (b) What cultures rarely use anything other than hands to eat?

Table 10.1 The dietary principles and practices of different religions

Religion	Dietary principles and practices	Forbidden	Fasting
Hinduism	Hindus believe that all living things are sacred and it is considered wrong to take another creature's life to sustain one's own. The cow is sacred. Devout Hindus are therefore vegetarian (eating no meat, fish or eggs).	Beef Alcohol	Often adults, normally women, fast for one or two days per week, often restricting food intake rather than complete abstention.
Sikhism	As Hinduism.		
Islam	These are laid down in the Muslim holy book, the *Qur'an*, and are regarded as the direct command of God. Meat must be **halal** (bled to death and dedicated to God by a Muslim present at the killing).	Pork and pork products Alcohol	All healthy adults must fast during the 30 days of Ramadan, eating and drinking nothing between dawn and sunset. The time of Ramadan changes with the calendar.
Judaism	Devout Jews adhere to the Jewish *kashrut* (dietary laws) as part of a code of discipline. Meat must be killed by the **kosher** method (the throat of a healthy animal or bird is cut quickly and the blood drained). The meat is then salted and steeped in water to remove all remaining blood. For the most orthodox Jews, meat and milk may not be used together in cooking and must be kept separate during preparation.	Pork and pork products Shellfish and any fish without fins or scales All foods containing yeast during Passover (March or April)	Devout Jews take no food or liquid for 25 hours at the feast of Yom Kippur (the Day of Atonement) in September or October.

Table 10.1 The dietary principles and practices of different religions *(continued)*

Religion	Dietary principles and practices	Forbidden	Fasting
Rastafarianism	Diet is very important. Rastafarians consider that the foods eaten reflect the health of the body and soul, and so only eat 'pure' foods. Additives and preservatives are avoided, canning of foods is thought to remove goodness, but frozen foods are acceptable. Most Rastafarians are vegetarian. They often prefer to eat in private.	Pork (some Rastafarians do eat other meat)	No specified times.

Note: Many Christian groups follow certain dietary restrictions at specified times. Sweet and rich foods are often given up during Lent. Buddhists sometimes refrain from eating meat on the days of the full and new moons.

Vegetarian, vegan and other diets

- **Vegetarian** – not eating food that comes from animals that involve them being killed, so for example milk, cheese and eggs are acceptable, but fish is not, sometimes the term lacto-ovo-vegetarian is used. Lacto-vegetarians eat dairy produce but not eggs.
- **Vegan** – not eating any food that comes from an animal source. For example, all animal meat, fish, eggs, milk, cheese, gelatine and honey are unacceptable. Remember, foods that have used animal products in processing are also unsuitable, for example cakes and biscuits use margarine or butter, soups may have a meat stock base and thus would not be allowed.
- **Demi veg** – a term occasionally used to describe people who eat little or no meat, but may eat animal products and fish.
- **Pescetarians** – people who eat fish but no meat.

Interest in vegetarian diets has increased during recent years. There are now thought to be up to 7 million vegetarians in the UK, of whom 250 000 are vegan. The reasons may be health, cultural or moral. In young children the decision not to eat meat is taken for them by their parents/carers as the providers of their food. A vegetarian diet can provide all the nutrients for a child's growth and development, but as in any diet variety and balance is needed. Children are often faddy eaters and need choices to get the essential balance in their diets; this might be more difficult for a child who does not eat meat or fish.

A vegan diet may present more challenges in ensuring healthy growth and development takes place. A mixture of plant proteins derived from cereals, peas, beans and nuts will provide sufficient good quality protein. However special care is needed to ensure that enough energy, calcium, iron and vitamins B and D are available. Dietary advice from a paediatric dietician may be required. A completely raw diet of vegan food (see Fructarian diet, page 167) is unsuitable and potentially fatal for a young child. An immature dietary system is unable to make use of raw fruits and vegetables that have not been broken down by the cooking process. The result could be severe faltering growth and possible starvation.

NUTRIENTS IN VEGETARIAN AND VEGAN DIETS

Protein

Milk and milk products are rich in protein, as are pulses, nuts and seeds. In addition, bread, cereals and potatoes are useful. Soya beans can be made into soya milk, cheese, yoghurt and ice-cream and are valuable in the vegan diet. Remember, however, that only animal source proteins contain all the essential amino acids (**HBV**), and plant proteins only contain a selection (**LBV**).

It is esssential, therefore, that variety is provided if animal sources are not included in the diet – this allows for the deficits in one plant protein to be compensated for by the amino acids in another, for example rice and bean casserole, and baked beans on wholemeal toast. These meals then contain HBV proteins. This is known as complementation of plant proteins.

Look back at Protein, Chapter 2, page 11, to remind yourself about high and low biological value protein (HBV and LBV).

Iron

Meat and meat products are important sources of iron, an area where children may be deficient. In a vegetarian diet it is therefore essential to include in the diet helpings of lentils, leafy green vegetables (such as spinach), dried fruits, peas, beans or tofu, accompanied by a source of vitamin C (orange or citrus fruit drink) to increase absorption of iron.

Calcium

Milk and milk products are excellent sources of calcium and to a lesser extent so are leafy green vegetables, tofu and soya milk, apricots, sesame seeds and bread. However, calcium from plant foods may be more difficult to absorb from the intestine.

Vitamin D

This is found naturally in a limited number of foods, all of animal origin. Oily fish is an exceptionally valuable source, so if fish is excluded from the diet children need to take their pint of whole milk daily and eat other sources where vitamins are added, such as breakfast cereals. Sunlight on the skin is the main source of vitamin D and very young children may need a supplement if exposure is limited.

Vitamin B_{12}

Milk and milk products are excellent sources of vitamin B_{12}, which is not found naturally in plant foods. However, breakfast cereals and yeast extract are fortified with this vitamin. Vegans will need to include a supplement to their diet.

Dietary fibre

Vegetarian diets potentially have a high fibre content, which is not always suitable for growing children (see Dietary fibre, Chapter 2, page 15).

PLANNING A VEGETARIAN DIET using four food groups, and fats and oils in moderation

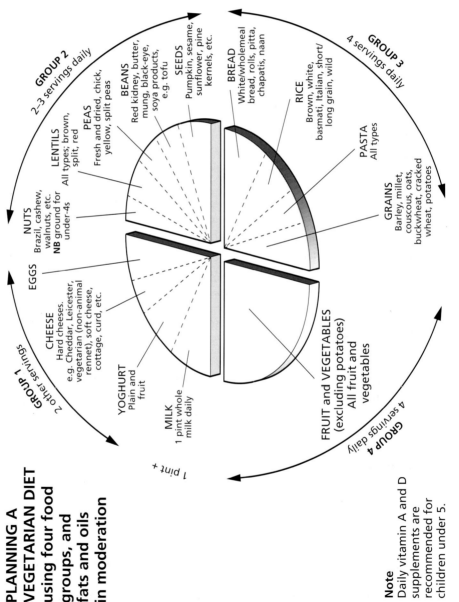

Vegans
- Exclude group 1 – additonal B_{12} supplements necessary.
- Portions from remaining three sections will require adjustment.
- Dietary advice will be needed.

GROUP 2
2–3 servings daily

BEANS
Red kidney, butter, mung, black-eye, soya products, e.g. tofu

SEEDS
Pumpkin, sesame, sunflower, pine kernels, etc.

PEAS
Fresh and dried, chick, yellow, split peas

LENTILS
All types; brown, split, red

NUTS
Brazil, cashew, walnuts, etc.
NB ground for under-4s

GROUP 3
4 servings daily

BREAD
White/wholemeal bread, rolls, pitta, chapatis, naan

RICE
Brown, white, basmati, Italian, short/long grain, wild

PASTA
All types

GRAINS
Barley, millet, couscous, oats, buckwheat, cracked wheat, potatoes

GROUP 1
2 other servings

EGGS

CHEESE
Hard cheeses.
e.g. Cheddar, Leicester, vegetarian (non-animal rennet), soft cheese, cottage, curd, etc.

YOGHURT
Plain and fruit

MILK
1 pint whole milk daily

1 pint +

GROUP 4
4 servings daily

FRUIT and VEGETABLES
(excluding potatoes)
All fruit and vegetables

Note
Daily vitamin A and D supplements are recommended for children under 5.

Planning a vegetarian diet

REMEMBER!

■ A high fibre content may impair the absorption of minerals. Extra bran must not be given.
■ When planning vegetarian diets look for 'hidden' animal products, for example stocks in soups, gravies, etc.
■ Make sure you understand the difference between vegan and vegetarian.

The chart on page 166 will help you with planning vegetarian and vegan diets.

DAY CARE AND DIFFERENT DIETS

When caring for a child whose diet is different from his peers, or unfamiliar to you, planning is important. Before the child is admitted to the setting, meet with the parents and learn what is, or is not allowed, and discover the child's own likes and dislikes. You may have to undertake additional research to update your personal knowledge. The admission of a child with a different diet may provide an ideal opportunity for a day care setting to widen the range of food offered. This might not always be possible so, as a last report, the individual child might need to bring his own food in daily, or on days when the food is unsuitable for his regime.

Eating in a group can be daunting for very young children and for a child seen as 'different' the minimum of fuss is essential at mealtimes. Ironing out any difficulties in advance will help. Parents should be confident their wishes are respected and valued.

DIETS UNSUITABLE FOR CHILDREN

Macrobiotic
This is a complex diet followed for philosophical and spiritual reasons. The diet is progressive and becomes increasingly restrictive. Progression takes place through ten levels, each eliminating more animal products, until the highest level is reached. This is a diet comprising only brown rice.

Fructarian
As a vegan diet but with avoidance of processed and usually cooked foods too.

SAFE PRACTICE

Both macrobiotic and fructarian diets are nutritionally inadequate to support normal growth in young children and should be discouraged. Protein deficiency, energy malnutrition, anaemia and vitamin deficiency have been reported in children who have been placed on such diets.

QUICK CHECK

1 Why may multi-ethnic diets be 'healthier'?
2 List five commonly used foods that originate from the following countries/continents:
   (a) Greece
   (b) Italy
   (c) India
   (d) Africa
   (e) China.
3 Which religions regularly have a fasting period?
4 How must meat be slaughtered to comply with Jewish religious traditions?
5 How can you ensure that children who are eating a vegetarian diet receive their necessary energy and high biological protein intake?
6 In what ways could you introduce iron into a child's diet if he is restricted from eating red meat?
7 What foods are forbidden during the Jewish Passover?
8 A child who is vegetarian no longer 'likes' milk or cheese. What foods could supply the missing nutrients?
9 What arguments could you suggest to help a 6-year-old child who is vegetarian and who is being encouraged by her friends to try a beefburger?
10 Why are macrobiotic and fructarian diets unsuitable for young children?
11 Which foods are forbidden to devout Hindus?
12 Describe Jewish *kashrut*.
13 What do you understand by the term 'pure' food for Rastafarians?
14 Which vitamins and minerals might be missing from a vegan diet?
15 What is Ramadan?

KEY WORDS AND TERMS

You need to know what these words and phrases mean. Go back through the chapter and find out.

complementation in plant proteins	macrobiotic
fructarian	Ramadan
halal	vegan
kosher	vegetarian

---

11 COOKING EXPERIENCES WITH CHILDREN

> **This chapter covers:**
> ■ The value of cooking
> ■ Organisation and management

The value of cooking

Young children enjoy being involved in household tasks and imitating their carers, so cooking activities are usually very popular, and can provide an ideal link between home and the setting. With increasing family pressures, more mothers working outside the home, and greater use of convenience foods, the opportunities for children to cook at home are often limited. Early Years settings, play settings and schools can provide children with a variety of cooking experiences in a safe and supervised setting. Healthy Eating is one of the key themes of the government's National Healthy Schools Programme – see Chapter 6 for further details. However, the Child Poverty Action Group feels that the teaching of food skills (nutrition and cooking) needs to be reintroduced into the curriculum as a compulsory subject area. Several other bodies, including the British Nutrition Foundation, support the need for children to know about healthy eating and understand the value of selecting and enjoying appropriate diets.

Cooking activities for children enhance many developmental and life skills and can offer a range of learning opportunities for children of different ages.

COOKING AND THE CURRICULUM

The Early Years Foundation Stage
Since September 2008, all Ofsted-registered settings caring for children from birth to 31 August following their fifth birthday have been required to deliver a curriculum framework known as the Early Years Foundation Stage (EYFS). Six areas of learning have been chosen to provide a specific framework for a variety of early learning goals. These goals are reached

Weighing and measuring at home

through a series of stepping stones. The early learning goals link, at the end of the Foundation Stage, to Key Stage 1 of the National Curriculum.

Cooking can be effectively used to promote learning in all six areas of learning, supplying valuable, relevant experiences that can support a child's learning.

Listed below are the six areas of the EYFS, together with a selection of relevant stepping stones, and ideas about how cooking activities may support the learning experience.

1 Personal, social and emotional development

Through cooking children can learn to co-operate and work towards a common goal involving teamwork, sharing and taking turns. They gain independence in accomplishing and repeating tasks and develop patience when waiting for cooking to be completed by, for example, waiting for a jelly to set, or dough to rise. There is the group discipline and responsibility of washing up and tidying away, followed by the feeling of achievement and pleasure in sharing food with peers. Children can begin to make decisions, predict outcomes and problem solve.

They learn how to use and care for cooking and eating utensils. Basic hygiene rules, such as washing hands before handling or eating food are reinforced, together with simple safety skills and knowledge. Cooking is a skill valuable to both boys and girls and can lay the foundation for life-long healthy attitudes to food.

It can be particularly effective for younger children. Tension can be released in pummelling and kneading dough. Sensory development is enhanced by feeling different textures, such as rough and smooth, hearing cooking sounds – boiling, sizzling, crunching and whisking, and by the pleasures of tasting ingredients – sweet, sour, bitter and smooth, and experiencing a variety of aromas.

Relevant associated stepping stones for personal, social and emotional development include:

- being confident to try new activities, initiate ideas and speak in a familiar group
- working as part of a group or class, taking turns and sharing fairly, understanding that there needs to be agreed values and codes of behaviours for groups of people, including adults and children, to work together harmoniously
- selecting and using activities and resources independently.

Role of the Early Years Worker includes:

- being a role model in handling food hygienically, washing hands correctly and promoting safety
- involving children in agreeing codes of behaviour when undertaking cooking and taking responsibility for their implementation
- giving children time to practise more difficult skills such as chopping, pouring, etc.
- acknowledging children's prior experiences and knowledge of cooking within their family setting.

2 Communication, language and literacy

Through cooking children can learn many new words by discussion and interaction with their peers and the adults involved. Songs and rhymes associated with food can link learning about food with memory and repetition, rhythm and beat, for example using stories like *The Hungry Caterpillar* by Eric Carle and *Eat Up Gemma* by Sarah Hayes, and with classic rhymes such as Humpty Dumpty and Little Jack Horner. Children can make shopping list with different writing scripts, label utensils and follow recipes from around the world. Books of photographs can be made of the cooking activity and photographic recipe cards will provide an ongoing resource, and stimulate discussion. Cooking activities can be role-played in a home corner, using a variety of eating tools, vessels and cooking equipment from around the world.

Younger children can extend their vocabulary with words such as more, less, balance, light, heavy, melting, thick, thin, etc., while older children will learn more technical words such as sediment, solution and fermentation, and to follow recipe cards. The adult involved will be able to support and extend the children's language by explaining terms, introducing new words, describing processes and naming cooking utensils.

Relevant associated stepping stones for communication, language and literacy include:

- interacting with others, negotiating plans and activities, and taking turns in conversation
- sustaining attentive listening, responding to what they have heard by relevant comments questions or actions
- extending their vocabulary, exploring the meaning and sounds of new words.

Role of the Early Years Worker includes:

- setting up collaborative cooking, or food related activities and helping the children talk and plan together about how they will begin, what parts each will take and what materials or ingredients they will need
- encouraging children to predict outcomes of the activity, for example how long it will take for the jelly to set or the cake to rise
- encouraging children to use new words associated with the activity and to ensure they understand their meaning. To promote discussion by asking open-ended questions
- remembering children need to describe what they are doing, in addition to carrying out their activity.

3 Problem solving, reasoning and numeracy
Through cooking children can learn a wide range of mathematical concepts, including counting, measuring, sorting, grading, calculating, fractions and area. They learn about weight and the different amounts achieved from similar weights, for example 1g fat compared with 1g flour. They can see an egg increase in bulk when beaten, and how cake and bread mixtures rise and expand when baked in the oven.

Preparing and using the ingredients according to a recipe teaches children about sequencing. Children can solve problems such as how to share food out fairly and how to position a cutter on rolled out pastry so that the maximum number of pastry circles can be cut out.

Relevant associated stepping stones for mathematical development include:

- counting, checking and weighing the numbers and types of ingredients involved
- using mathematical concepts in weighing and measuring – more, less, heavier lighter, adding and taking away
- using emerging mathematical ideas and methods to solve such problems such as too much liquid, absorption, freezing, etc.

How many cake cases to fill the baking sheet?

Role of the Early Years Worker includes:
- helping promote a positive and fun approach to mathematical ideas, through cooking
- acknowledging that children have a natural interest in numbers, shapes, measuring, etc. and aiming to stimulate this
- posing relevant questions, for example 'what will happen if...'how can we make this...' 'what shape will this be...'
- promoting the 'doing' rather than the outcome of the activity.

4 Knowledge and understanding of the world

Through cooking children can discover about the range and extent of different foods and where they come from in the world. Children can investigate how food grows, and is produced. They can learn what plants need for growth and how this can be accelerated or hindered, for example climate differences, and the effects of too much or too little water. Awareness of food poverty and famine can be raised.

Learning can be reinforced by growing their own plants to cook and eat, ranging from simple cress on damp paper indoors, beans and potatoes in outdoor garden areas, or exotic vegetables in a growbag on a sunny terrace. They can develop an understanding of the seasons and the different length of time plants take to grow. They can also learn what parts of plants can be eaten, which foods are eaten raw and which cooked, and that certain foods, such as some berries and fungi, might be dangerous. The children can be introduced to the idea that foods can be used in a variety of ways – an apple can be sliced, chopped, stewed, baked or put in a pie as a dessert, or used with meat to complement savoury tastes.

Science concepts too are learnt, usually by 'doing,' for example the effects of heat on food, fats changing into oils, jelly and sugars dissolving, and water altering when it is heated or frozen, or evaporating when boiling. In the oxidation process children will see the effects of leaving an apple cut and noting the changes, and comparing the results with the appearance of the apple when dipped in lemon.

Cultural diversity can be celebrated in the setting through understanding about food varieties and diverse traditions, and by preparing, presenting, tasting and growing different foods. Parents from different cultures can be invited to cook foods within the setting, widening the opportunity for all children to taste unfamiliar foods, acknowledging the importance and contribution of different ethnic groups and forming a link between home and school. Visits to local restaurants could be arranged.

The involved adult at cooking time

Relevant associated stepping stones for knowledge and understanding of the world include:

■ selecting the tools and techniques needed to cook effectively – e.g. whisks, rolling pins, cutters

■ finding out about their environment and talking about those features they like and dislike – this could include how animals are reared and cared for, how plants are grown for food

■ beginning to know about their own cultures and beliefs and those of other people – this could include family feasts and diverse food traditions.

Role of the Early Years Worker includes:

■ providing the opportunities for children to discover their environment, including visits to farms, allotments and street markets

■ providing multicultural resources for cookery, and by valuing and reflecting cultural diversity in choice of foods and recipes and equipment in the home corner

■ ensuring wide access to cooking for children with different abilities, and by adapting techniques and equipment for children with special needs.

5 Physical development

Through cooking children can learn to enhance their fine manipulation skills by pouring, chopping, beating, screwing, unscrewing, mixing, slicing and stirring. Dexterity, control and hand–eye co-ordination are helped by pouring without spilling, separating egg yolk from white, and carefully filling cake cases. If children are involved in growing plants outdoors, their gross muscle power can be improved through digging, carrying, bending and stretching.

Relevant associated stepping stones for physical development include:

■ showing awareness of space, of themselves and others

■ using a range of small and large equipment

■ handling tools, objects and malleable materials safely and with increasing control.

Role of the Early Years Worker includes:

■ talking with children about keeping healthy while acknowledging that there are many things they do not control

■ allowing children to practise their physical skills through repetition and the use of tools

■ teaching them to use tools and materials safely and effectively.

6 Creative development

Through cooking children can learn to develop both their individual and group creativity. There are endless opportunities, and these can include choosing colours, designs and patterns to ice and decorate cakes and other foods, making different shaped biscuits. Group creativity could include setting tables and creating pleasant eating areas through using a range of patterns, colours and shapes of cloths, plates and napkins. Children can make food interest tables and share dishes that the group or individual has produced. They can co-operatively create wall displays to show where food originates, using drawings and pictures, and visit art galleries to see foods represented by famous painters. They may possibly create collages from dried foods or bags of pasta, although some settings feel that an awareness of the precious and scarce nature of food to many of the world's children does not make this option acceptable.

Relevant associated stepping stones for creative development include:
■ exploring colour, texture, shape, form and space in two or three dimensions
■ using their imagination in role-play and stories about food and cooking
■ responding in a variety of ways to what they see, smell, touch and feel.
Role of the Early Years Worker includes:
■ providing the opportunities, supervision and support for children to cook and create safely
■ supporting children in their choices
■ giving constructive feedback to their efforts and activities.

REMEMBER!

If using dried peas or beans careful supervision will be required. If placed in the mouth and inhaled there is a possibility of choking. They should not be used with children under 3 years, children with certain disabilities including learning disabilities and challenging behaviour. Only use these foods with close supervision for children aged 3–5 years. Most settings have a 'no nut' policy (see Chapter 3, page 41).

Activity
1 Plan and implement a biscuit making and eating session for a group of children aged 4–5 years.
2 How could you link this activity to each area of learning within the EYFS?
3 What is the role of the Early Years Worker in this activity?
Before planning this activity read Personal preparation and The cooking session, page 177.

Beyond the Early Years Foundation Stage
Key Stage 1 (5–7 years)
Food and nutrition is not designated as a statutory National Curriculum subject, and so it is rare for actual cooking activities to take place. However, many of the principles can be taught through other subjects, particularly

in science. There are additional opportunities through personal, social and health education and citizenship, although this is not mandatory. In view of this separation of the topic, a cohesive approach by the teaching team is needed to give a comprehensive understanding of the subject. Food and nutrition skills gained can provide an important link to the Healthy Schools Programme (see Chapter 6, page 94).

The Key Stage 1 curriculum areas that can be specifically linked to food and cooking are as follows:

- *In science* children should be taught:
  - that humans and other animals need food and water to survive
  - that taking exercise and eating the right types and amounts of food helps humans to keep healthy.
- At this stage children should begin to:
  - know that there are a wide variety of foods and that choice is based on needs and culture
  - know that food is needed for health and growth and that some foods are better than others.
- In personal, social and health education it is advised that children should be taught how to make simple choices that improve their health and well-being.

A variety of activities aimed at extending and developing these curriculum areas are suggested by the Health Schools website at www.healthy-schools.gov.uk. Suggestions include:

- learning about the Five Food Groups and linking them to growth and development
- raising awareness of diverse eating habits
- using sorting activities to show the different food groups
- keeping a food diary or charting the frequency of what has been eaten
- devising a food alphabet and looking at how many foods come from each food group
- discussing favourite foods from each group and collecting examples for display
- tasting and exploring foods from different food groups
- investigating what food is stored in refrigerator and what in a cupboard
- looking at two plates of different foods for breakfast, lunch and supper, and identifying the healthy, balanced choices.

For more ideas, visit www.nutrition.org.uk and follow the links to the Cook Club recipes for primary school aged children.

Key Stage 2 (7–11 years)

As children grow and develop they become increasingly aware of the world around them and their role in it. Learning about healthy eating and diet can encourage problem-solving, decision-making and help change dietary habits and behaviour. By 7–11 years (Key Stage 2) a child could be expected to:

■ know that diet is a combination of foods, each with different nutrients
■ know that nutrients have different effects on the body, and the amounts in the diet and balance between them, can influence health
■ know how to handle foods safely and recognise the importance of additives in food safety.

Suggested activities, to support and complement food and nutrition, could include:

■ discussing the food groups and the relative proportions of each needed to provide a balanced diet
■ investigating family meal patterns, family eating habits, roles of family members in shopping, preparing and cooking food and ethnic influences
■ conducting surveys of favourite foods, or eating behaviour, e.g. 'what we had for breakfast/lunch'
■ designing a board or card game based around food choices and nutritional value
■ investigating food preparation and storage
■ exploring the wording on packaging, including looking at organic and genetically modified food products.

REMEMBER!

The quality of the learning experience will depend, to a large extent, on your ability to explain, question and answer the children as the cooking takes place.

Organisation and management

Planning and organisation are vital and safety must be paramount. No more than four children under 5 years, or six children between 5 and 7 years, should take part in a cooking activity with one adult. The children not involved in cooking will need a different activity so they are not getting in the way and posing possible safety hazards. List the children not involved so they can have a chance next time.

PLANNING

The cooking activity you decide upon will vary depending on the setting, the facilities available, and the ages and numbers of children involved. You need to be aware of the dietary needs of the individual children, and you may need to adapt your plans for any child with a particular need, especially a child with poor co-ordination or learning difficulties.

You may be free to choose what cooking activity to do, or you may need to complement any existing plans in the setting. In a class in a school there will probably be an ongoing topic or theme, but within a home as part of a daily routine you might be able to select your own activity. A school or nursery class, with a long-term topic such as 'Warm climates', could provide opportunities for the children to shop in a street market for ingredients to make an exotic fruit salad or colourful ratatouille, allow children to make lists and negotiate money and change. At home a simple activity may be making sandwiches for lunch, offering useful pre-maths work with quarters and halves of bread, or possibly making hot cross buns for tea. This will give scientific information about the concepts of fermentation and the effects of heat.

Whether planning a formal or informal activity, always consider the six areas of learning in the Foundation Stage and plan how you will extend each of these. It is useful to write down:

■ what you want the children to learn and what attitudes, skills and knowledge will be addressed

■ your own preparation – what you need to research, learn, provide and organise. You will need to practise first too, at home or college

■ how you plan to record the progress of each individual child – the skills and knowledge they achieve.

REMEMBER!

Consider the parents'/carers' cultural and moral wishes regarding food for their child, both in handling and eating food. Consider fillings for sandwiches – for example ham would be unsuitable for children who are Muslim, Jewish or vegetarian.

Activity
What dishes could be prepared in the following circumstances:
1 no source of heat?
2 boiling water only?
3 hot plate only?
4 full oven facilities?

Developmental considerations
Children develop rapidly during the early years. However, each child is an individual and may have particular strengths and weaknesses in different developmental areas. As an Early Years worker you should know the children individually in order to plan for and meet any special needs. You must also consider the age and skill range of the whole group with whom you will be cooking.

■ *Children aged 2–4* – plan for limited concentration. Waiting for bread to rise, cakes to cook or jelly to set may be difficult at this age and quicker results will be required. Physical strength for pouring and beating will be limited.

■ *Children aged 4–6* – at this age more sophisticated concepts can be introduced. Children can now wait for the transition of a cake mix into a sponge or the chopped vegetables into soup.

■ *Children aged 6–8* – children will now be able to follow a recipe card with simple written or pictorial instructions. Concepts of fermentation in bread-making and the extended process of two proving periods would now be tolerated. The cooking activity can link in with work on the National Curriculum in maths, science, history, geography and English at Key Stages 1 and 2.

■ *Children with special needs* – consider whether adaptations are needed, such as wheelchair access to the cooking area, modifications to equipment and large print recipe cards. Will you need additional help? Perhaps a parent could be invited in for the cooking session?

The chart on page 181 summarises all the points you will need to consider when planning a cooking session.

Preparation of the children

■ Discuss the reasons for a chosen recipe. Involve the children in the planning, for example by reading books to discover the origin of unfamiliar ingredients.

■ Explain the safety rules clearly and fully.

■ Ensure their hands are washed, nails short, no rings, hair tied back and clean aprons. Explain that they should not taste food without your permission, nor should they eat food that has fallen on to the floor.

■ For maximum fun and learning, everyone must be involved and 'doing', not just observing, so sufficient equipment, bowls, spoons, aprons etc. for each child will be needed.

■ Children could do their own measuring, counting and weighing, working from recipe cards they have been involved in designing.

GOOD PRACTICE

■ Does your planning consider the individual needs of everyone in the group?
■ Is there a 'healthy eating' message in your recipe?
■ Is there a realistic savoury and sweet balance in your recipes?
■ Are you introducing foods from different cultures?
■ Are you using a variety of flavours, tastes, textures and smells?
■ Provide encouragement and support: praise efforts; take time to explain and interact; observe reactions; remind about 'independent tasting'.

Extend and develop your planning by:

■ thinking how you can involve, welcome and value parental support. Always remember any parental group will have a wide range of expertise and experience that would enrich a cooking activity

■ considering how you can extend a simple cooking activity into other areas, for example food for a picnic or celebration

■ following up the activity, possibly by outings to local restaurants or cafés.

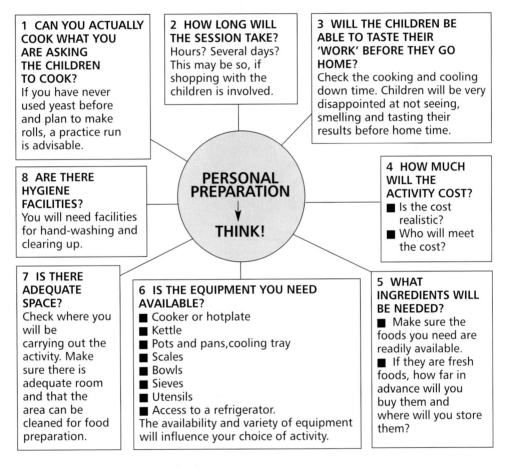

1 CAN YOU ACTUALLY COOK WHAT YOU ARE ASKING THE CHILDREN TO COOK?
If you have never used yeast before and plan to make rolls, a practice run is advisable.

2 HOW LONG WILL THE SESSION TAKE?
Hours? Several days? This may be so, if shopping with the children is involved.

3 WILL THE CHILDREN BE ABLE TO TASTE THEIR 'WORK' BEFORE THEY GO HOME?
Check the cooking and cooling down time. Children will be very disappointed at not seeing, smelling and tasting their results before home time.

8 ARE THERE HYGIENE FACILITIES?
You will need facilities for hand-washing and clearing up.

PERSONAL PREPARATION
↓
THINK!

4 HOW MUCH WILL THE ACTIVITY COST?
■ Is the cost realistic?
■ Who will meet the cost?

7 IS THERE ADEQUATE SPACE?
Check where you will be carrying out the activity. Make sure there is adequate room and that the area can be cleaned for food preparation.

6 IS THE EQUIPMENT YOU NEED AVAILABLE?
■ Cooker or hotplate
■ Kettle
■ Pots and pans, cooling tray
■ Scales
■ Bowls
■ Sieves
■ Utensils
■ Access to a refrigerator.
The availability and variety of equipment will influence your choice of activity.

5 WHAT INGREDIENTS WILL BE NEEDED?
■ Make sure the foods you need are readily available.
■ If they are fresh foods, how far in advance will you buy them and where will you store them?

Personal preparation – think!

The cooking session

Liaison with the nursery team will be necessary as cooking may need to be undertaken with several groups over a period of days so that no child is left out.

- With your group, collect all the ingredients and equipment needed.
- Ensure your cooking area is clean and free of clutter.
- If an oven or other source of heat is to be used, check the safety procedures and remind the group of the rules.
- Supervise weighing and measuring, both for accuracy and to reinforce counting and measuring concepts.
- Ensure that all the children see the different stages taking place – 'rubbing in' when making pastry, the stages of elasticity in bread dough and the proving process, the effects of liquid on dry ingredients and how quickly the jelly melts with varying temperatures.
- Teach the children to use equipment correctly – how to cut with sharp knives, use peelers and beaters, how to estimate timings on a microwave oven. These are all useful life skills.

How many pastry rounds from one large circle?

SAFE PRACTICE

Whenever heat is used in a cooking activity you will need to decide what is safe for children.
- The use of hot fat and frying are unsuitable activities for young children.
- An adult can open an oven to let a child place her cooking inside, but the child must be protected with oven gloves.
- Children should not be allowed to light a gas oven with matches. They may, under supervision, operate a gas oven with automatic ignition or an electric oven.
- Pouring boiling water requires muscle power and co-ordination and mishaps can be serious. Adults must always undertake this task.

Teaching children how to keep safe in a potentially dangerous area like the kitchen is an important aspect of any cooking activity.

FOLLOW-UP WORK

Everyone needs to be involved in the clearing away and washing up. Think what you are going to do with the food that has been prepared/cooked. Suggestions might include:

■ letting the children take the food home if suitable containers are available
■ laying the food out on a prepared table and making a special occasion of it for all the children in the nursery or class
■ setting up a shop in the home corner (decide on your 'currency')
■ inviting parents/carers to see and taste the results of the children's work
■ record the individual children's achievements, skills and knowledge
■ encourage follow-up activities, including science tasks, story/songs linking to curriculum projects, research into where specific food originates, food chains and growing food.

SELF-EVALUATION

■ Do you think that the session you organised went well?
■ What changes, if any, would you arrange for another occasion?
■ Did you manage to involve all the children and did they participate fully?
■ How accurate was your timing?
■ Did you extend all areas of the learning process? Look at your skills and language check list.
■ How could you assess whether the children remembered what they learnt in the session and how could you reinforce the learning?
■ Make a list of the new words you felt were introduced to the children, by you, during the activity.
■ Did another worker observe the session? Did he or she have additional comments that would help your personal assessment?

Finally, keep the recipe in a resource file for the nursery or class, adding any comments and amendments for future use.

Activity
Research a variety of different religious festivals.
1 What special foods are offered during these occasions?
2 After liaison and discussion with the nursery staff, plan and implement an activity to cook one of these foods. Remember the developmental stage of the group. You will need to prepare the children about the

background and reasons for the foods being prepared. How will you do this? Would it be appropriate to involve parents/carers who have special knowledge of the festival foods and their traditions?

3 Prepare your menu cards.
4 Take your group out to buy the necessary ingredients.

QUICK CHECK

1 What gross and fine motor skills can children gain from cooking?
2 Describe the science concepts that can be introduced during a bread-making session.
3 What possible outcomes or predictions could you pose to a child when making jelly?
4 How might you introduce maths when making sandwiches?
5 How could you develop sensory awareness when cooking with children with special needs?
6 List 20 new words associated with cake making that you could introduce.
7 How can cooking lay the foundation for a healthy attitude to food?
8 How could you best meet the different developmental needs of two groups of children, one aged 4 and the other 6 years, when planning a cooking activity?
9 What cooking activity might you offer to a child with a visual impairment?
10 How could you reflect a multicultural approach to cooking with young children?
11 Why is it important for all children to be involved and not just observing when cooking?
12 What safety factors are essential when using an oven with a group of children?
13 List the plans you would make for a cake-making session with a group of three 3 year olds.
14 What social development can take place during a group cooking activity?
15 Why is it important to check the gender balance of children involved in cooking sessions?

KEY WORDS AND TERMS

You need to know what these words and phrases mean. Go back through the chapter and find out.

The Early Years Foundation Stage (EYFS)

Key Stages 1 & 2 Food and Nutrition

Early Learning Goals

The six areas of learning

Stepping stones

GLOSSARY OF NUTRITIONAL TERMS

Allergy   A severe reaction to a particular food

Amino acids   The chemical structure of proteins – compounds of carbon, hydrogen, oxygen and nitrogen

Colostrum   The first important milk produced by the breasts, rich in protein and antibodies

Curd-dominant formula milk   Baby milk containing the protein casein, for the hungrier baby

Dairy foods   Milk (from cows, goats and sheep) and foods made from milk – butter, cheese, cream, yoghurt

Dehydration   Loss of water from body or food

Dietary reference values (**DRVs**)   Recommended nutrient requirements for different groups of individuals

E numbers   Numbers given to food additives approved by the European Union (EU)

EFAs   Essential fatty acids

Empty calories   Energy obtained from single nutrient foods, particularly sugars, sugary foods and drinks

Enteral nutrition   Providing nutrition into the gastrointestinal tract via a tube

Energy   Essential fuel for all body processes

Enzymes   Special proteins needed for all chemical reactions in the body

Fluoride   A trace element that protects tooth enamel

Faltering growth   Failure to gain weight and grow as expected

Food groups   Foods grouped according to their main nutrient content

Fore milk   The milk at the beginning of a breastfeed, which is high in lactose

Fortified foods   Foods that have vitamins and minerals added, such as breads and breakfast cereals

FSA   Food Standards Agency

Gluten   A protein found in cereals such as wheat, barley, oats and rye

Glycogen   The name given to glucose stored in the liver and muscles

Haem iron   The most readily absorbed dietary iron

Haemoglobin   A protein in red blood cells, which carries oxygen around the body

Halal   Meat from animals slaughtered according to Islamic (Muslim) religion

High biological value (HBV)   Proteins found in animal foods and containing all the essential amino acids

Hind milk   The milk that follows the fore milk, rich in fat (calories)

Hydrolysed protein   A specially adapted formula milk used in allergy management

Insulin   A hormone produced by the pancreas necessary for carbohydrate metabolism

Intolerance   Inability to tolerate a certain food, usually short-lived. Signs and symptoms may include vomiting, diarrhoea, rashes and failure to thrive

Irradiation   A method of preserving food using gamma rays

Joule/calorie   Measurement of food energy

Kosher   Meat from animals slaughtered according to Judaism, the Jewish religion

Lactose   Milk sugar

Let-down reflex   The mechanism, in breast-feeding, by which milk is squeezed out of the milk cells into the milk ducts

Low biological value (LBV)   Proteins found in vegetable and plant foods containing only some essential amino acids

Macronutrients   Nutrients that supply energy and are needed in large amounts – proteins, fat and carbohydrate

Metabolism   Describes all the changes that take place in the body to do with food and energy use

Micronutrients   Nutrients needed in small amounts – vitamins and minerals, which do not supply energy

Moulds   Invisible tiny plants on food surfaces, which cause food spoilage

Non-haem iron   The less well-absorbed dietary iron

Nutrients   The building blocks of food, which provide material for growth and maintain good health

Pancreatic enzyme   A digestive juice produced by the pancreas. It can be manufactured artificially

Parenteral nutrition   Providing nutrition directly into a central vein in the body

Pathogens   Harmful organisms

Phenylalanine   An essential amino acid

Polyunsaturated fat   Fat, mainly from vegetable/plant sources – may lower level of blood cholesterol

Preservatives   Natural or artificial additives used to prolong the life of food

Protein   A macronutrient essential for growth and repair of body tissue, can be animal or plant source

Protein complementation   Combining a variety of LBV protein foods to ensure all essential amino acids are obtained

SACN   Scientific Advisory Committee on Nutrition

Saturated fat   Fat, mainly from animal sources, linked to coronary heart disease

Socio-economic   Classification of families by their social status and level of income

Soya milk   Milk produced from the soya bean

Staple foods   Foods that form the bulk of a diet

Tartrazine   An orange colouring added to sweets and drinks

Unavailable carbohydrate   The term used to describe fibre – carbohydrate that does not nourish the body but is necessary for good health

Vegan   A diet that excludes the eating of animal flesh and products

Vegetarian   A diet that excludes the eating of animal flesh

Well-balanced nutrition   A daily diet that includes a wide variety of foods from the food groups

Whey-dominant formula milk   Baby milk nearest in composition to breast milk, containing the protein lactalbumin

Yeasts   Micro organsims that can cause food spoilage, but are used in fermentation, for example in breads and alcohol

USEFUL CONTACT ADDRESSES AND WEBSITES

Note: When using the internet, select your information carefully and remember that not all sites supply information that has been supported by wide research and academic scrutiny. Government and established charities are excellent sources, providing comprehensive, current information.

beat
103 Prince of Wales Road
Norwich NR1 1DW
Tel 08456 341414
www.b-eat.co.uk
Charity offering information and help on all aspects of eating disorders, including anorexia nervosa, bulimia nervosa and binge eating disorder. It also provides a telephone helpline.

The Breast feeding Network
PO Box 11126
Paisley PA2 8YB
www.breastfeeding.org.uk
An independent source of support and information for breast-feeding women.

British Nutrition Foundation
High Holborn House
52–54 High Holborn
London WC1V 6RQ
Tel 020 7404 6504
Fax 020 7404 6747
email: postbox@nutrition.org.uk
www.nutrition.org.uk

Child Growth Foundation
2 Mayfield Avenue
Chiswick
London W4 1PW
www.cgf.org.uk
Research and information source for all conditions affecting children's growth.

The Children's Society
Edward Rudolf House
Margery Street
London WC1X OJL
www.childrenssociety.org.uk
A nationwide children's charity involved in a variety of projects, including current research on faltering growth.

Child Poverty Action Group (CPAG)
94 White Lion Street
London N1 9PF
www.cpag.org.uk

CPAG Scotland
Unit 425, Pentagon Centre
Washington Street
Glasgow G3 8AZ
www.cpag.org.uk/scotland
CPAG is a leading organisation campaigning on all issues concerned with children and poverty.

Children Living with Inherited Metabolic Disease (CLIMB)
Climb Building
176 Nantwich Road
Crewe CW2 6BG
Tel 0800 652 3181
www.climb.org.uk
Umbrella organisation working on behalf of children, young people and families affected by metabolic disease.

Coeliac UK
3rd Floor, Apollo Centre
Desborough Road
High Wycombe HP11 2QW
Tel 01494 437 278
www.coeliac.org.uk
Raising awareness of coeliac condition and offering support, information and advice. The society provides a current UK food list to members with information about gluten-free products.

Cystic Fibrosis Trust
11 London Road
Bromley
Kent BR1 1BY
www.cftrust.org.uk

Diabetes UK
Macleod House
10 Parkway
London NW1 7AA
Tel 020 7424 1000
www.diabetes.org.uk
Leading charity working for people with diabetes providing information,
support and advice.

Food Commission
94 White Lion Street
London N1 9PF
www.foodcomm.org.uk
Independent watchdog over food issues including quality, safety and education.

Health Information East London
81–91 Commercial Road
London E1 1RD
Tel 020 7655 6685
www.hiel.nhs.uk/public
Tower Hamlets NHS Trust produce leaflets and video material in multiple
languages, including weaning information in Bengali. *The Balance of Good
Health* is available in Bengali, Chinese, Gujerati, Punjabi, Somali, Turkish,
Urdu and Vietnamese.

Islamic Food and Nutrition Council of America
5901 N. Cicero St 309
Chicago, IL 60646
www.ifanca.org/halal
The Islamic Food and Nutrition Council of America (IFANCA) is a non-
profit Islamic organisation dedicated to promoting halal food and the insti-
tution of halal.

La Leche League
Tel 0845 456 1855
www.laleche.org.uk
Help and information for women wishing to breast-feed their babies
and personal counselling to mothers having difficulties with breast-feeding.

London Beth Din Kashrut Division
Head Office
Kashrut Division
735 High Road
London N12 0US
www.kosher.org.uk
Lists up-to-date information on kosher food products and establishments.

Maternity Action
The Grayston Centre
28 Charles Square
London N1 6HT
www.maternityaction.org.uk
Organisation producing a booklet for mothers combining breast-feeding
with returning to work. Material covered includes practicalities and legal
rights and how to negotiate with employers.

National Society for Phenylketonuria (NSPKU)
PO Box 26642
London N14 4ZF
www.nspku.org
Information, advice and support.

National Health Service
Foods Standards Agency (FSA)
www.food.gov.uk

and

Department of Health (DH)
Marketing Communications
Skipton House
80 London Road
London SE1 6LH
www.dh.gov.uk

Schools Health Education Unit
Renslade House, Bonhay Road
Exeter
Devon EX4 3AY
www.sheu.org.uk

SCOPE
6 Market Road
London N7 9PW
www.scope.org.uk
Charity in England and Wales concerned with disability issues, especially cerebral palsy.

The Vegan Society UK
Donald Watson House
21 Hylton Street
Hockley
Birmingham B18 6HJ
www.vegansociety.com
The Vegan Society aims to promote healthy living for the benefit of people, animals and the environment.

The Vegetarian Society
Parkdale
Dunham Road
Altrincham
Cheshire WA14 4QG
www.vegsoc.org
Advice for people wanting to follow a meat-free diet.

Websites with current and relevant information

British Dental Health Foundation
www.dentalhealth.org.uk
Charity dedicated to raising awareness of all aspects of dental health. Website has useful links to other relevant bodies.

British Nutrition Foundation
www.nutrition.org.uk

Change4Life
www.nhs.uk/change4life

Department for Children, Schools and Families
www.dcsf.gov.uk/schoollunches

Food Standards Agency
www.eatwell.gov.uk
Government agency set up to protects consumers' rights and interests in relation to food quality and safety.

Healthy Schools
www.healthyschools.gov.uk
Government site for teachers.

National Institute for Health and Clinical Excellence NHS
www.nice.org.uk

Nutrition and School Lunches
www.direct.gov.uk.en/parents/schoolslearninganddevelopment/schoollife/DG_4016089

QCA: Qualification and Curriculum Authority
www.qca.org.uk

School Food Trust
www.schoolfoodtrust.org.uk

INDEX

Page numbers in italics indicate tables and diagrams.